AND THEN I KNEW
MY ABUNDANCE

Lessons from *A Course in Miracles*

James Nussbaumer

For permission, serialization, condensation, adaptions, or for our catalog of other publications, write to Ozark Mountain Publishing, Inc., P.O. Box 754, Huntsville, AR 72740, ATTN: Permissions Dpartment.

Library of Congress Cataloging-in-Publication Data

Nussbaumer, James – 1957 -
And Then I Knew My Abundance by James Nussbaumer

This book is concerned with making contact with the effective and purposeful part of the mind where the confusing possibilities about your consciousness are cleared away, and the absolute is brought forward. Imagine a place of insightful activity that you're able to find somewhere in your mind— This place exists. It's where your true potential can once and for all be realized, and then accepted.

1. Manifestation 2.Co Creation 3.Power of Thought 4. Metaphysical
I. Nussbaumer, James, 1957 - II. Metaphysical III.. Title

Library of Congress Catalog Card Number:2017964440
ISBN: 9781940265506

Cover Art and Layout: www.vril8.com
Book set in: Times New Roman, Papyrus
Book Design: Tab Pillar
Published by:

OZARK
MOUNTAIN
PUBLISHING

PO Box 754, Huntsville, AR 72740
800-935-0045 or 479-738-2348; fax 479-738-2448
WWW.OZARKMT.COM

Printed in Canada

To my Father and all those faces in the crowd he taught me to deeply consider.

Contents

Introduction

Imagine a place of insightful activity that you're able to find somewhere in your mind—a place where the confusing possibilities about your consciousness are cleared away, and the absolute is brought forward. This place exists. It's where your true potential can once and for all be realized, and then accepted. As your curiosity plays alongside doubts, reaching the ever-widening boundaries of your thoughts, you are able, if you so choose, to reestablish contact with the Source of the active center of what gives you life.

This book is concerned with making contact with this effective and purposeful part of the mind. You will learn to realize your consciousness in a different way from the familiar way it may have been making you operate in the physical world. You will learn to recognize consciousness as an entity that you create, but do so from behind it. I know this may seem confusing, so for now, and just to buffer the impact of this thought about "*you being behind your own consciousness*," allow me first to ask you to consider a couple of extending thoughts. By extending I mean sharing our Reality together as One.

Ask yourself, what is truly a higher order: the physical or our natural Divine Self? If separated from nature the mind becomes a hollow bundle of shallow thoughts, lacking all activity, without luster and authenticity, seeking only projected images seen as form, and without the pleasure of being real, or, let's say Divine. I do realize we're just beginning our journey together through this book, but for now consider a projected image being something the world has taught us to see since our birth into this world. Something your physical past has taught you to picture in your mind.

Imagine a physical experience, like hearing the ringing of the opening bell on Wall Street, and then imagine a natural experience, like hearing a wood hen hammering as it hollows out an oak tree, the sound echoing through the forest. When you compare the two, you will note the two different portrayals consciousness gives us to consider. One is a reflection through your body's eyes, and the other is simply a gratifying vision. Which one is real?

For now the question might provoke confusion, because the way the world teaches us makes us initially think that both are real. But that's okay; at least I've got your perceptive mind's eyebrow raised. With that, let's consider how you feel about this world.

Have you ever felt that the world around you—all that you see through the air, land, and sea—just doesn't seem to be home? Or, phrased differently, that something feels like it's missing in your life, but you can't seem to pinpoint it, or even narrow it down? How often have we all said, "I wish I could find myself," or "I just can't seem to touch what has been bothering me?"

You may experience such a stage in your life that passes with the help of time, but then with more time that "lost" feeling arises again. Your experience tells you that nothing is different in the way you feel, other than this time you are older. The situations or circumstances going on around you may divert your attention for a while, until the lingering memory or sense of a greater reality comes back to haunt you and seems to own you. You still feel lost or like an alien from somewhere unknown. It's as though you are here in exile. This may be a subtle feeling that surfaces every now and then, sometimes nothing more than a tiny throb, and at other times a blur that is hardly remembered—actively dismissed, but persistent and sure to return.

No one ever figures out where this place might be that has claim to your naturalness. Many try to shrug it off, or hide their suffering in dreams, or in games they play to occupy their time and keep their sadness suppressed. Others will deny any such feelings and not recognize or admit their fear at all. And most people will maintain that what I speak of here is a figment of the imagination. Yet who, in simple honesty, without being defensive and self-deceived, would deny he understands what I mean?

Is There Really Any Stability I Can Achieve?

This book is for everyone who walks this planet and who wants to understand that it is okay to be seeking something stable, because you surely are lost and seemingly not at home. The individuals who seek out the many messages this book offers have been uncertain, in an endless search through the fog for what he or she cannot seem to find, while not recognizing that they already hold onto it. Striving continues for the perfect family and home, the career, cars, the vacations, and all the toys, which are all fine, and you should enjoy these things. Yet none of this gives contentment to our restless mind, with one thing for sure: the fear of death and hell, and believe it or not, the fear of the gate to Heaven.

If you're like I used to be, you wish you could return to your childhood so you could have a chance to do things differently. You know, that younger body, that old neighborhood—maybe with the ongoing ballgames in the backyards, running through the lawn sprinkler on hot summer afternoons, or building a snowman in the front yard in the winter. All of this is only a memory, like a dream you once had, so distorted that you can barely hold a picture of it now.

As you find your way through these pages, you may find it to your advantage if you've already read my two previous books, *The Master of Everything* and *Mastering Your Own Spiritual Freedom*. If you haven't read either, however, that's okay, because I've written this book while considering those who lack the information in the previous books, and this book will help first-time readers when you do get a chance to read the others.

My goal in this book is that you will come to know the part of you that accepts yourself as an alien in the world. Your home is the childhood all around you, which is eternal, with an innocence that calls the shots while you're here walking around this land. This real and true childhood is your Divinity and brings to Earth a pure reflection of "why" you are here. In that reasoning of "why" is the spotlight that has already shone its intended purpose onto you, and now all you need to do is simply play out the role. It's really that simple, with nothing to fear.

While living in the Light you'll know your way and will no longer feel lost, because you will discover you are innocent of everything. All fear and guilt will fade. Your goals are not a figment of your imagination, but are real, if they are your heart's desire.

Your imagination is the voice that tells you to lay down all defenses and let the child within you lead the way. His home is yours. The gate is not to be feared and the way is open to you. The only figment of your imagination has been the world's blockade that you've allowed to hold you back, along with the obscuring fog limiting your vision of this Light.

You've already taken the first step by opening this book, and in the pages ahead simply walk the gentle way while fearing no evil and no shadows in the night. Both are unreal.

I welcome you to the journey with all that I can be.

James Nussbaumer

PART I
THE DREAM OF LIFE

Chapter 1
The Jewel

In a remote realm of perfection, the kingdom was suddenly bereft. There ruled a just and all-loving monarch who had wonderful children, and they lived in happiness together as a loving family. One day the father called to his eldest child with something extremely important to say.

"The time has come, my dear son," he announced, "to complete what has suddenly left our kingdom wanting. I am sending you away, an infinite distance, to another land. You shall seek and find and bring back the precious *Jewel*."

The son traveled in disguise to this strange land, whose inhabitants almost all lived in darkness. Such was the effect of this place that the child lost touch with himself, wandering around in a daze as if only partially awake.

From time to time he saw phantoms, and similitudes of his homeland and of the Jewel, but such was his condition that these things only increased the degree of his daydreaming, which he now accepted as his reality.

When news of his son's plight reached the king, he sent word to the son by a trusted messenger, a Guide, who possessed a wise spirit blessed by the king. The Guide located and approached the son. "Remember your purpose here," he told the lad. "You must begin to awaken from your reverie and find your way."

With this message the son roused himself, and with the help of the Guide, the son dared to face the monstrous perils that surrounded the Jewel. But by the miraculous powers within the Jewel, the son easily returned to his realm, to remain in increased peace and happiness forevermore.

You have these miraculous powers of the Jewel deep within yourself, as do we all, and it is a treasure of incalculable value. Because the power and strength of the Jewel is within, you are that Jewel. If you can realize and accept this fact, you will come into a permanent endowment of knowledge, revealing and extending your true identity to others so that they too may realize this in their own selves. You will come to know yourself and become confident as to why you are here. Just as this ancient parable is said to contain all wisdom in its various levels of interpretation, so do you contain this truth within you.

What Actually Is an Interpretation, Anyway?

Idries Shah, the foremost contemporary exponent of Sufism, was once asked to name a "fundamental mistake" that most individuals make, and his response sparked my thinking about my own interpretation of reality. He answered that "Our errors rest in the fact that we think we are alive, when we really have fallen asleep in life's waiting room, which is the illusion most of mankind is influenced by."

In a similar discussion about man's destiny, a Zen master added, "It is the ordinary state of consciousness we call *'waking'* that is so far from our seeing things as they truly are, that it could more accurately be called *'sleep'* or *'dreaming.'*"

The philosopher Bertrand Russell has written, "The dreams we call waking perceptions have only a very little more resemblance to objective reality than the fantastic dreams of sleep."

Think about it. How do you really know that you're awake right now? Could it be because the world tells us, "Of course you are awake. Why would you argue this fact? Are you nuts?"

You may say you remember waking up from your last night's sleep. But that may merely have been a "false awakening," and you might be fooling yourself now by actually being in a dream that is telling you it's not a dream. Perhaps what we take to be "true awakenings" are just another degree of partial or false awakenings.

So once more, now, try to really ask yourself this question: Am I really awake?

You will note within yourself how difficult it is to genuinely raise the question. A part of you says that this is a ridiculous thought. However, to even ask sincerely whether or not you're really awake requires honest doubt—a willingness to accept "no" for an answer, even if the amount of doubt and willingness is tiny. Or is there an urging inside of you that is asking this? Inside, you are aware that if you try to believe this you'll feel some guilt, due to the idea seeming ridiculous. This is no easy matter for most of us. But also consider, if the idea does seem ridiculous to you, how did this notion get seeded into you?

Please move on now, and as you do, seriously ask yourself about all of this again, and then again. How might we not be fully awake? If this is so, could it be that we possess a higher sense—such as a type of intuition, let's say—that ordinarily remains asleep, when our lesser, though better-accepted senses are awake?

Additionally, the daily experience we call "waking up," and consider to be complete, may in fact only be a partial awakening. This is the case in what is called "*lucid dreaming*," where part of us is consciously awake while another part of the mind dreams while asleep. This alone has been a deep subject that has undergone countless research studies by so-called dream experts. Or could we just call them expert dreamers?

All kidding aside—and please take my comment lightly—notice that even in your own dreams there is usually a character present whom the sleeper, *you*, takes to be yourself. It's through the dream eyes of your dream body that you normally witness the events of the dream. The dream body is usually who we think we are while dreaming, and this seems an obvious conclusion. But we actually are only dreaming of being that person.

The dream character is merely a representation of ourselves—or we can call this the *dream ego*, as the actor of the dream. The point of view of the dream ego is that of a willing participant, apparently contained within a multidimensional world (the dream), much as you probably experience your existence at this moment, while you read and think about this possibility.

Chapter 2
Humanity's Vicious Circle

Wouldn't you agree that a dreaming mind is made by thought and expressed in form, and then projected sort of like a movie? A dreaming mind does begin with a thought that is totally separate from its true reality. Without a reality, the thought and the dream must, of course, be unreal.

The strangest dream that humanity as a whole could ever dream continues today, and includes thoughts of fearing God. I say here "humanity as a whole" because man's complete entity, or system, which must be the mind and not the body, derived from a more Supreme Mind, which extended Itself in thought, an activity known as the Creation. Symbolically we call that very first extension, in bodily form, Adam—a word that means humankind.

The Bible tells us that Adam—all of humankind—fell into a deep sleep before Eve's casual conversations with the serpent. Nowhere, however, is there a single reference to his/her waking up. How could there be? Humanity must still be asleep. A dreaming mind can only either dream about one day awakening or simply awaken, with the dream being ended. If Adam did awaken, wouldn't it have been discussed and written about, especially in the Bible? When the mind does awaken, wouldn't it most likely be a slow and natural process, one of comfort and ease, rather than an abrupt jolt? I believe so; any other way would be forced and wouldn't be natural. That is, of course, if it's a sweet dream instead of a nightmare.

While you allow that to sink in, there's more to consider. Somewhere along the line the very first thought, ever, to separate from its Source, or Reality, can be considered a projected image onto the movie screen of life, making an identity of flesh and bones. From that point on, thoughts proliferated. In the Garden of Eden, on what seemed to be a spring morning, all sorts of thoughts gave birth, sending perceptions of doubt, fear, and guilt zinging through the air to form further images, in a process of thought that would later be termed "consciousness."

This consciousness, or conscious mind, continues to dream and is the projected image of time and space. The images appeared as a seeming reality, and oceans were suddenly breaking ashore, accompanied by a misty, obscuring fog. Seagulls and pelicans and all other wildlife had not realized humanity's fall to the knees of guilt. These creatures, as well as plant life, were brought to the dream as symbols of something natural, giving humankind a sense of the certainty of a naturalness to which it was connected in the reality behind the dream. We can call this the naturalness behind consciousness.

This nature became the changing seasons, which humanity dreamed up to project the tick of time. Through the fog many other images compelled themselves, as consciousness continued to usher in more and more space to accommodate the panoramic picture. With the continued projection of guilt, painful changes began to be ordered onto the horizon.

Making History

As humanity's first few conscious thoughts, in the symbolic form of Adam and Eve if you'd like, exited paradise, their real home, the first separated minds were hit hard with shame and regret. Their guilt-laced thoughts of separating from the Oneness of eternal bliss plagued them. But they would never come to accept that it was only an error in thought that ignited the dream of a frightening future, and they continued to search for a way out of the fog. Keeping their eye on the future and dwelling on the past, generations to follow in their footsteps would continue to repeat more errors, thus making history. The errors would consciously, and then religiously, be labeled as sin.

Although merely a separated thought, and nothing more, is what makes the dream, the guilt attached to this error has snowballed to be seen as the mountain of sin on which we live.

To this day humanity as a whole still dreams of sin and has failed to realize that through time, our erroneous zone for processing thoughts is being reversed in an ongoing, effortless process by the power of true reality. This process is our Divinity, slowly helping us to awaken from the dream of sin. Being a dream, sin is not real and is the illusion we live by. Can it be that our dreamed-up authors of this illusory form of life also developed a thought system to fit the picture? The projection of sin seems to be the vicious circle by which we live.

For now much of the world sees this as a fearful thought that keeps us frantically searching the drama for something "out there" that may save us. But accepting the error as just that, an error, is all it takes to undo the process. This "undoing" is the reversal necessary so we can comfortably, without pain, awaken to our true reality of inner peace.

Look at it this way: Hallucinations fade away when they are faced head-on. All that we project seems to have fear attached to it in some form. Then we further project a cost of sacrifice in order that we may rid ourselves of the fear.

By going along with this we get nowhere. It's the strangest belief man has ever made in the dream of separate identities. We've been taught to think that our Source, which I call God, is angry because of our errors, when all along this has been nothing more than a wishful fantasy of the way we look at the world. We believe if we focus our fear long enough, the pain seen as sacrifice will eventually reward us with salvation. This is why, in order to be looked upon as righteous, we think we need to be considered a "God-fearing" individual.

This type of conscious thinking is an example of wrong-mindedness, where wrong perceptions and thoughts make up wrong ideas in a mind that dreams it is split apart, or separated from its original Source, or God. But keep in mind that the word "wrong" is not to be interpreted as "bad." Rather, wrong-mindedness is simply erroneous.

Projecting Images

Wrong-mindedness consists of thoughts and perceptions that establish the fear we live by. We can call this the "dream ego" or simply "the ego." The ego is the false idea of who we are—the illusion of separate identities or selves. It identifies itself with the false or illusory, but it is not intentionally bad. It's an error that needs erasing or correction without punishment. When it is corrected we see the innocence that always existed.

Try to see that the ego in itself is not evil or bad, although bad types of images certainly do emerge from the ego. If God's Will is His Creation, the innocence that we are *behind* the ego must also be God's Will. If we are afraid of His Will then we must be fearful of ourselves. This is why we continue the façade by wearing the mask that frightens us when we see its projected image. It's as though we work at being afraid, and in so doing we are afraid of our own shadows.

To add even more confusion, doubt, and fear to this illusory thought system the ego gives us, the guilt we carry for believing in it is so deep we don't realize it, and it splinters into even deeper fragments as we try to defend it or hide it. An example of this is in all of the thoughts you have when you either bury the truth or try to make up your own truth, and then try to defend that in your thoughts. This defensive reaction makes us even more fearful, so we cling more fiercely to even more fantasy till the bitter end—which stops at our tombstone. The ego's thought system tells us to dream, and that the end—our death—is where we will find salvation.

But salvation from what? The ego in each of us cannot truly answer this question without doubt. How can we survive after death if we have a thought system separated or split off from that of our Source, who created us of itself, a thought, and the only real thought that exists? Any such separate thoughts or beliefs could not possibly have occurred unless part of the mind became divided due to a false idea, or wishful thinking. This is what has left us doubtful and afraid of a questionable reality.

What is it we really question? How can what is not of God be real? And if God has no fear, how can our own fears be real? Fear must be a separated, unreal thought, an illusion. If we are of God, how did we acquire this fear, when fear certainly is not of His Will?

The answer is simple. Each fear we have arises from the wrong-minded thought system we think makes us into who we are. This must tell us that fear is only a dream-thought and doesn't exist in the real world behind the movie screen of our life. Fear can only be a false belief—but it's the illusion that runs our lives. It's our separated state of mind, the ego, that insists fear is real, and that our bodies are all that we are. If we turn off the projector, take the screen down, and turn on the light, what do we see? We see Reality.

If doubt, fear, and guilt are nonexistent, then what does exist? Only you do. Without you, there is no projection or movie screen to reflect images, which means there would be no world around you. You are the Idea of the One Mind of all existence that is eternally real beyond such projections. God created you, but only you generate the projections. The real world has no separate parts. It is this wholeness that sustains each of us without limitation. There is not a single projected image to see within wholeness. But while we dream of duality and images that seem to begin and end, we've been given a Guide to help us see these projections for what they merely are.

Chapter 3
The Dream Character, or Ego

When someone compliments you and is lovingly sincere in doing so, by telling you what a *jewel* you are, do you think they are talking about your flesh and bones? Of course not. They are referring to the treasure that is you.

If we are all of the "likeness" (Idea) of God, then other ideas or thoughts are clearly fantasy. They are a wrong-minded, or erroneous, approach in perceiving what we think we are, more properly understood as what we *wish* to be—what the ego wishes us to be. Only when we perceive through our right-mindedness can we understand fear for what it is: the confusion and uncertainty of wrong-minded vision, which is unreal. Think about this:

When your heart makes its final beat and lungs release that final breath of air, and your body is surely deceased, where is fear then?

Any true free will you have cannot be of wrong-mindedness, where total attention is always on the body. This is why the ego resists any type of right-minded perceptions. Right-mindedness is also perception based, but is too positive and too real for the ego, with minimal attention given to the body. This makes the ego cower as it turns its face in the opposite direction. We have all cringed this way when we've caught a glimpse of our own positive nature, as well as that of others. But once the perception sinks in, we think, *Hey, maybe there's truth to this.*

Your Protector

In a psychological, rather than religious, context, the right-mind is host to the Spirit of God, which throughout this book I will refer to as the Holy Spirit. (I refer to God using the masculine Him and He only for convenience.) God's Holy Spirit, or His Thought, is holy in a psychological sense because it is of your true essence. The essence of anything is its holiness. We'll talk more about this later, but for now try to see the word "holy" as merely a word, a few physical letters of the alphabet that do not need to be sprinkled with special water. It's the meaning behind the word I want you to be concerned with, not the word itself, or the ego's interpretation.

The Holy Spirit will use the laws of the ego-based world, which is unreal, to get your attention if He must. It is these laws the ego, or wrong-mindedness, is afraid to examine; whereas right-minded perceptions and thoughts have a willingness to sense that the dreamer (you) is safely asleep at Home.

The right-mind carries a strong perception or sensation that you are protected from eternal doom and gloom. It senses there is no such thing as hell. Have you ever had those moments of pure peace, comfort, joy, and love, where everything seemed to be going in the right direction? Sure you have, and this is it! This is where the right-mind outweighs the wrong-minded side of the split-mind in your daily, moment-by-moment thoughts and perceptions.

In this state of mind you still may observe slight or background fearful thoughts, but they are easily overlooked by the security of the Holy Occupier of your right-mind. What seems to be the "fear of God" is your own ego's guilt for seeing itself as only a body.

Keep in mind as we move along that your right-mindedness is the step below the One-mindedness of Creation. God extends Himself through the right-mind as you carry on the dream of separation. The erroneous wrong-mindedness of the dream itself could never have even a glimpse of wholeness, because the ego is unreal. Only what is real can have sense, and wholeness certainly is sensible. Think about it. It's pretty difficult to find any truth in all that makes no sense to you, and comes at you from different directions, and makes you feel confused and anxious.

Being so, the ego-mind feels itself lacking; panic sets in, so it's difficult to learn or receive anything that wishes to abandon the unreal for the real. This constant feeling of "lacking" sows confusion in us about who we truly are. The fear is the ego's reluctance to accept the fact that we do indeed have a true essence. The ego is aware that it can never be a part of it, or come to know it.

All the ego can do is to one day fade away or be obliterated once the body is deceased and begins turning to dust. Even this "turning to dust" notion is an attempt by the ego to believe it has a bit more time, when actually the ego is gone in a flash once the brain has stopped. But in reality, the ego only dreams of all this. Its life is only a dream and has no afterlife.

This is what is truly meant by "from dust to dust shall you be."

This truth is why, for the most part, we don't take kindly to change. We are actually afraid of our real self and the real depth of others, which is the wholeness of God. This notion frightens us and thus makes the ego feel safer. The ego likes to see us as "god-fearing" individuals, not part of any whole. It keeps us in line with its way of thinking, and it gives some folks the feeling of being "holier than thou."

Chapter 4
The Ego will Try to Surround Your Reality

It might seem funny that we're not aware of our true reality. But shouldn't it be even funnier that we're so sure it's fearsome? Think about it: We're so afraid of things it's . . . well, scary. But if you are serious about getting a grip on this fear stuff, you must begin to accept that truth and fear cannot coexist. If you are afraid of something, it means you are not being truthful with it.

When it is faced with the truth, the ego stops laughing. It doesn't know what to do next when it sees itself caught up against truth. It can only make up excuses as it turns away, shaking its head in feigned disgust.

We think there is something beyond what we see, but we also think we don't want to know it because it is frightening. But what we are really doing is judging something that has not yet arrived. We believe we must escape from what has not yet captured us. Is this funny, or is it crazy?

Your Guide Will Sort Things Out

Regardless of the ego's insanity, we must not forget that we do have our Guide to clear the insanity out of the way. The Holy Spirit will sort things out for us because He actually knows what our reality is. For example, my guidance asks me to build a foundation in the first half of this book so the remaining half will lead to a conclusion that will open your eyes to your true capabilities—through His Guidance. Through stories of my experiences, you may see, in your own unique way, the reality of the world, regardless of ego-based thought.

Why does this work? The Idea that you are of God has already been created. Now, while you dream, your Guide will use time to bring your purpose to the projection screen that you call your life. As the role is played out and your purpose in life is being displayed, you are slowly and comfortably reawakening, until the lights go on in the theater and the picture show is over. At that point in eternity, where all you see is ego-free wholeness, you will no longer need the Holy Spirit because you will realize that He is you.

Until total reawakening has occurred, however, the Holy Spirit will be your Dream Weaver. The task will be to constantly and consistently interlace a pattern for you that leads to the accomplishment of your true free will. He is not attempting to force a function on you, but He is strengthening and bringing your attention to what it is you truly want. His task is to place it into your awareness, which also abides in your right-mind. All truth about you rests there. You may ask, why do we need to have a free will? We will go into more detail about this later, but basically it's necessary so we can help others, as well as ourselves, to awaken naturally.

Bear in mind that the ego is persistent in its efforts to surround your free will outside of your awareness, so that your free will may not seem free at all. This is where, at times, it may seem as though your true purpose is inside the body, encased in or surrounded by the brain. This is ego-based thought controlling you.

This is evident when you feel imprisoned by a job, or a relationship, or a direction that you feel is off-track, or any number of factors that can occupy your daily living. Your fears are your captors and keep the Jewel about you hidden. With the help of your Guide, you can see through the falsities of the fog-obscured path. This is your journey, though because of the fog you may not have been able to look at it this way.

The Magnitude of Your Real Vision

By not being on the outside, but on the inside of your mind, the Holy Spirit has the power to look at everything you have hidden away and to alert you to the Will of God that circulates there. The Holy Spirit is you—the aspect of you that sees through the Spirit of God the wholeness of all that is real. The dreaming portion of your mind, which has illusively split away, is extremely tiny when compared to the vastness of your whole mind and is not the real you. It is fabricated in its littleness.

The infinite depth of what you really are has the reality to not be affected by any such tiny obstruction. Your real vision, being infinite, is of a magnitude that will never be matched, no matter how much the littleness of the ego builds its forces. And besides that, you must remember that your dreaming ego-mind is not real.

With this fully understood, or even partially understood due to some ego-based obstruction, try to remember, or at least keep in the back of your mind, the unreality of the ego. You may have some resistance, but that's normal; consider it to be okay for now. As you travel through this book, try to see any ego chatter as background static, kind of like bratty kids in the neighborhood simply trying to get attention, but whose antics don't really bother you.

The Holy Spirit is continuously roaming around your entire mind as you dream of separation. This includes even the fragmented, splintered, and split-apart areas where He watches over your fantasy thoughts of a separate will, which you have been seeing as your life. In this area of your mind He sorts out the truth from the false.

As we previously discussed, however, much of the depths of your mind is not dreaming. This is the whole, unseparated, knowledgeable, and truthful *real* you behind the dream, which has the power to instruct the dreamer to dream in a direction of your true free will. When all of humanity as a whole can live its true free will, the ego will have totally faded away and the result will be total reawakening. This is the process the Holy Spirit is involved with now, in a slow, comfortable pattern drawn around your state of willingness and readiness at any particular moment.

However, the ego, out of fear, is diligently working hard to resist any unseparated notion. Why? Because the ego needs fantasy and knows nothing else. This is why, in its own defense, it will talk to you about "taking it to the grave." Of course this type of mindset makes anything real, and of truth, seem frightening.

The Barrier to Full Awakening

The Holy Spirit is your reality, and the ego is not, but tries to be. We said earlier in a different way that the Holy Spirit instructs your right-mind to perceive a direction for awakening that includes your free will, or purpose, or function. But for the time being, we all individually must only partially awaken, gradually, a little bit at a time. For all of humanity to come through the barrier of separation to full awakening as One Mind, the wholeness itself must accept the entire idea of God's Will being Creation Itself.

The one Idea of Creation is the one Son of God. We can interpret this as His only "begotten son," called the Sonship, as in "relationship" to oneness. This does not entail a physical body or a gender. The Son of God, or Sonship, is all minds, whole, which bodies can never be or even project an image of. The images projected of a body are always subject to change. Wholeness does not change.

When the knowledge of the Holy Spirit brings your reality to you, or shows you your purpose, He is helping you to remember what you are, and this does not change, even while you dream of changing times. The side of you that feels it is lacking is also fearful of what it "might lose." The dreamer in you does not understand, however, that the Holy Spirit in you sees only what you are truly meant to have and to be. Peace is what you are truly meant to have, and truth is what you are meant to be.

The Holy Spirit will never call upon you to make a single sacrifice of any kind, but the ego will. Sacrifice is not part of the peaceful path to awakening, and if you insist, you are listening to and taking advice from your fearful separated mind. This is the same thought system that may have taught you of an actual real, physical body called Adam, and then Eve, a loving couple being "driven" by an "angry God" from an actual location called Eden. Do I mean to say that none of this ever existed?

Sure it existed, but only in the dream of projected images, where the ego insists they were real. The ego places blame for its "lack" on the loss of "paradise" described in this wishful fantasy. But what does the ego actually lack? That's easy: It lacks reality.

Your Guide, the Universal Inspiration, reminds you that sacrifice is not God's Will for you. There is no cost for having a life of purpose. This is why it is a true *free* will.

Once the mind of humanity can understand this split between reality and the dream world of separate identities, then we will recognize that our purpose and the process of living out this purpose is our real salvation—not a fantasy paradise outside of ourselves. When this inner peace is discovered where it has been all along, within us, we will then know that salvation is not needed. Why? Because we will have already been saved.

Chapter 5
The Two Thought Systems

A dying man lies on an emergency room gurney. As he reaches the point of greatest physical distress, he hears himself pronounced dead by the doctor. He begins to hear an uncomfortable noise, a loud ringing or buzzing, and at the same time feels himself moving rapidly above his own physical body. Though still in the same immediate physical environment, he sees his body from a distance, as though he is a spectator. He watches the many resuscitation attempts from this vantage point and experiences a state of emotional upheaval.

After a time, he collects himself and becomes more accustomed to his condition. It is reminiscent of something familiar. He notices that he doesn't have a body any longer and realizes he is now limitless, possessed with powers his body never realized. But these powers are not new at all, and now he remembers them from before he ever had a body, before his physical birth. This adds to his already tremendous bliss.

Some other things begin to happen. Others who are also of a limitless nature arrive to greet him and join him in the same blissful existence. He has glimpses of the spirits of relatives and friends, and all those he read about in history books, and these glimpses turn into a unified presence. He is at-one with all of them, as a single peaceful presence.

He notices a shared loving, warm, and gentle white light that envelops him, yet is limitless. At some point he finds himself approaching some sort of barrier or borderland, apparently representing a limit to particular thoughts. This borderland reveals to him that he is able to go back to Earth if he so chooses. All he must do is simply look to the past and relive the appropriate bordering, past thoughts. He sees that the thoughts themselves will send him back. But without hesitation he resists, and rather chooses to be taken up with the experiences of being safe at Home.

His choice not to return is enough. He is overwhelmed with intense feelings of joy, peace, love, and contentment. He is convinced in that instant, which seems to be all there is in the definition of time. The running together of instants is a Oneness he accepts called eternity.

Age of anything is nonexistent and has no meaning, as he realizes eternity is the only real time he has ever had, and now ever will have. He discovers that all of the unreality he perceived and participated in while on Earth was the obstruction to the time he now has available to himself.

Truth Knows What It Wants

A Course in Miracles states as the nineteenth of its fifty precepts that "Miracles make minds one in God. They depend on cooperation because the Sonship is the sum of all that God created. Miracles therefore reflect the laws of eternity, not of time."

As you enjoy this book, please try to keep in mind this *ACIM* principle. But do so casually, much as you would keep in mind that the kids are safely buckled up in the backseat while you are driving on a long road trip. You witness the changes in the landscape as you get nearer your destination, all the while knowing your passengers, your loved ones, are safe.

Have you ever been in a situation in which you felt everything was 100 percent truthful, and peace was the result? Similarly, peace cannot occur without faith. When we commit to truth as our only goal, we are guided to truth by faith. The faith I speak of here is not belief in a particular religion. The faith to which I refer encompasses everyone involved, which allows the situation to be perceived as meaningful only because it is whole. Truth is whole. Think about how many parts to truth you can dissect and talk about. You can't do it, because truth is all it ever can be; it is one.

Truth and illusion, or false ideas, have no connection whatsoever. This will remain forever true, regardless of the utmost efforts put forth by the ego to try to make the untrue into something even remotely true. Nothing is ever partially true. All illusions, however, are connected to each other. They are seen as separate wholes against each other, whereas truth stands as one, with nothing in its way. Truth and illusion each have their own thought system, but they are not connected or related to each other in any fashion. Truth knows what it wants, whereas illusion makes promises for the future.

Your Extension to Others

To perceive these two distinct thought systems, it would make sense that we recognize truth and illusion as indeed separate from each other. The result of any idea is never separate from its Source. An idea of anything being separate from its Source is a thought produced by the body, derived from the past, and is not a real idea. The result is always nothing: lack of attainment of a goal that was never possible. The Source is always a part of the result for it to be real.

A good example here is my love and passion for the game of golf. I have played and practiced this sport all my adult life, starting in my teens, and I have been considered to be a fairly good golfer. No matter how hard I grind at perfecting my average golf score, however, and no matter how diligently I work at each and every aspect of this difficult sport, I know within myself that I am limited. This is not wrong-minded thinking. I am positive in the knowledge within me that I will never be able to compete with the top guns on the PGA Tour. I will never be breaking the records held by the all-time great golfer Jack Nicklaus. For me to set out on a path to do so would not be God's Will; it would be illusory wrong-mindedness.

On the other hand, I also love to write, and write at length, as in "writing books," especially about what I have learned on my spiritual path. This is an area where I know in my heart I can truly excel, while helping the fine individuals who take an interest in what I have to pass along. I am able to spend hours on end at the writing table and truly love it; to me it doesn't seem like work. It gives me immense inner peace to extend myself in this way.

Will I ever win a Pulitzer Prize or any other type of achievement award due to my love for writing and my willingness to teach? That of course I don't know. It is not my goal to be a prize-winning author, but I don't rule it out, either!

My point here—and please consider this carefully before moving on—is this: What idea or pursuit can you possibly have that you extend to others, and that will have a result totally separate from you? And if you do see it as a separate result, is it separate from *you* or from your body? Is there even a difference in how you perceive this? If you give the idea away, isn't it still your idea? Jack Nicklaus broke many records that he holds to this day, that others enjoy and aim for as their own goal in improving their level of performance.

Now I do not compare myself to Jack Nicklaus, but just as he has done with golf, I give you this book so you may incorporate my ideas into your own, helping you to look at life in a way that may bring you inner peace, as it has done for me. Of course you must use my ideas in a way that suits you. We can say that my ideas become your ideas as you expand on them, make them better, and extend them to others. This is wholeness at *play*—not work.

Let's consider the importance of your faith in the "idea." To have faith in something is to heal, or to make whole, because it reveals its truth. Your own healing is a sign that you have accepted yourself as whole, as being a part of or joined with something true and good, not erroneous. Don't get me wrong; errors will come along as they always do on the way to perfection. Just ask Jack Nicklaus how often he had to make adjustments to his swing mechanics.

When you're on a path with something true and exciting, you sense the feeling of wholeness as your Source. What heals becomes whole, and faith allows for healing—the idea of being free of the past—and believe it or not, you will feel the freedom from the confinement of being stuck in a body. It's this freedom that directs you along a path within your Source, and this is God.

Faith is natural and cannot be forced. Ask Jack Nicklaus what most likely will occur when he tries to force his golf swing. Faith is the opposite of fear, but is as much a part of love as fear is of forcing a situation. Faith is your acknowledgment of union, and it is what keeps you united with your one and only Source.

Consider the power of electricity as it flows through the wiring on its way to the light switch. There is one continuous flow from its source—a gapless, unseparated flow, or extension. Faith is the flipping on of the light switch that lets you see yourself as you are now, always now, and it has no use for the past.

Chapter 6
Jailer or Liberator? It's Your Choice

Does it surprise you that *real faith* will only represent what is true? It shouldn't surprise you at all, and is why the opposite—no faith at all, or faithlessness—is nothing more than fear trying to make its untruths into what it wishes to be seen as true.

Faithlessness will always place limits and attack in some form, or will try to force itself into a situation even if it's in thought. Faith, however, removes all limitations and brings in wholeness. Faithlessness will destroy and separate, while faith will unite and heal. Faithlessness will make up false ideas of yourself, expecting them to turn true, and then struggle against what you truly are. But it's impossible not to be the same as your Source, which is God's Will for you, and nothing removed or exaggerated.

Your faith in this idea removes the obstacles that make you seem to be separate. Truth is the absence of false ideas about yourself, and truth is your freedom. It's your false ideas about yourself and the world around you that make you struggle in life. But to dedicate yourself to both truth and separateness is to set up a goal forever impossible to attain, because much of it is sought after by the body and for results only of the body.

An example of such a false idea is that I could become a record-breaking golf professional. The way of healing such false ideas that call upon the mind can easily be handled by a corrective thought process, for example: "I would like to spend the years ahead participating in golf at a peak level appropriate and rewarding for me, and whatever results that come about are fine for me. Meanwhile, as I have fun with golf, I will pursue my writing ability with a goal to offer a message that will serve others." This example is an attitude that heals and thus is true participation in wholeness. Being involved in wholeness sets you free.

Faithlessness Leading to Illusion

Don't overlook the fact that faithlessness leads directly to a fantasy purpose you are not meant to attain. You'll never arrive, and likely respond with disappointment, frustration, guilt, and anger. Faithlessness does have its purpose, however. A lack of faith will indirectly help you toward the truth, by leading to that ever-prevalent, confusing question: Why am I here?

Due to the forces that are brought forward by faithlessness, a segment of the mind chooses to see itself as separate from the Universal Purpose, which is awakening. With this false idea the body becomes the instrument of fantasy. It acts on seeing what is not really there and hears only what it wishes to take from a situation, working to make that true. Ask yourself: How many times have I tried to *help* a matter be seen as true, or truer, or truest?

All real purpose draws on real faith and is easily exchanged for the knowledge of what is real. For instance, don't you truly know when you pretend to have knowledge on an issue, especially in a group discussion? That's okay; we've all done this. At least it proves where your true knowledge lies: inside.

This may give you a slight chuckle; such posturing in order to appease the ego is all too human. But this teaches us that faith arises in each of us from the Universal Inspiration as a perception that eventually bridges its way to inner knowledge, and this depends on our individual readiness at any given time. Try to mentally picture your positive, right-minded perceptions as the building of a bridge over the valley of ego-based nonsense to true knowledge. By doing so you will begin to see faith as a gift—an "idea" of inspiration given to you by your True Self. Then you will become ready to say to yourself, *Ahh, of course. Now I know why I'm here!*

This becomes an uninterrupted state of bliss, which is your *holiness*. It doesn't require that you receive it or accept it by wearing special garments, using special oils or water, or being involved in special ceremonies. Holiness does not come to you in this way. These are all fine if this is what comforts your body temporarily. But that's all these types of things can do for you. These actions do not prove yourself to be a spiritual person. Miracles and magic are not related, because one is real and the other unreal.

Grace is not given to a body, but is forever holy in your mind. "Holiness" is a word that is often assigned a deceptive meaning by the ego, a meaning steeped in magic or a quality bestowed from "out there." But holiness has a true meaning: Your mind receives and gives always as different aspects of the same thought.

This true idea, or understanding, of being holy is what gives you faith. It's in your spirit or inner urging that is willing to look beyond the body. This action is the real definition of forgiveness and is what heals. Healing removes illusion from the mind and makes whole what thinks it is separate.

You can enslave a body, but an idea is free and incapable of being kept in prison, or limited in any way, except by a mind that wishes to see false ideas. Ideas travel from mind to mind within an ocean of wholeness called Spirit.

Your spirit remains joined to its Source, and whether you see a jailer or a liberator depends on which thought system you choose to live by. Do you wish to struggle at chasing after fantasy, or do you want to be guided to the reality of your true existence?

Chapter 7
The Secret Society

There is a group of individuals from the past, present, and even those who have not yet arrived into the dream of life, who know how to use their minds. It is a secret society of minds representing the eternal One-mindedness we ultimately are, as well as the right-mindedness of humanity as a whole. This unity of minds affirms an affinity within humankind while keeping the world from destroying itself. These minds have another way of looking at the world.

Many of you will begin to pick up on this soon by recognizing it in others you encounter in everyday life. Some of you will also immediately become alerted to minds of past beings and those not here yet. In some manner they are all a part of the wholeness of humanity's tiny segment of mind that dozed off for a while and dreams. The ones who are not here yet merely have not yet projected themselves onto the screen of life. But in everyone, regardless of their projected-image status, is the true oneness behind the dream that is eternally existent. For those who are deceased, those of us presently here carry their weak projected image around with us in our physical memory.

This secret society is a group of real minds who understand and can glimpse a sense of connectedness to all that exists beyond the physical world. Throughout this book, as you read, you will most likely realize you have at one time or another found yourself sensing this same connectedness or unity.

In no way, fashion, or form is this infinite society to be considered a cult, because that would require an idol to follow or worship. When the only guidance is Truth, which needs no worshipping, an idol means nothing. This society of Truth is esoteric in nature, basically meaning that its true essence does not require or rely on advertising, with its mission being to begin to accept responsibility for humanity.

The society shares its inner realm of inspiration with all of reality. When, or if, our bodies ever meet, we may or may not recognize one another as such, but usually it doesn't take long before we realize each other's spiritual presence. But as you will see ahead, often we reveal ourselves in other ways that are not actually physical or even conscious. These meetings could be direct or indirect, through a television or radio show, the Internet, a book, a letter in the mail, or any other means of communication humanity shares.

The Membership

Anything that is free and has a mission of helping others in order to save the world automatically raises an eyebrow of doubt in the ego in each of us. But please begin reading with mostly your right-mind now—the positive nature in you that wants the best out of life while you're here. The only catch to this secret society is that any wrong-mindedness holding you back from your true potential will be caught up in a right-minded wind and blown away.

Membership is open to everyone who is a truth-seeker, and your commitment is not validated, nor is any form of documented enrollment required. In fact, it is unheard of. Some are more wholly and deeply involved than others, but at these different levels everyone senses their own unique function.

Keep in mind that without absolute truth one could never have such a sensation, which is not always knowledge at first, but often quickly shifts into an exciting acceptance of one's path. There is, however, a certain urging or voice, if you will, that speaks to others who are ready to lend support.

This society of peace and wellness and forgiveness has been doing a profound kind of thought processing for thousands of years. It includes, but is not limited to, for example, Jesus, the Buddha, St. Thomas, and average men and women from all walks of life, and a whole line of others who were known or popular, like Mother Teresa, Pope John Paul II, Abraham Maslow, Einstein, and many more. Their names and bodies don't matter because they eventually wither, but minds remain as an idea that time will never abolish.

You've seen these individuals everywhere, on a local level as well as worldwide. You know who they are. From the volunteers at hospitals and nursing homes to the young individual who shoveled your driveway before dawn, without notice or expecting so much as a thank-you. These people act in these ways out of kindness of heart that the body cannot understand.

They have a mission in a mind that abides behind their own consciousness.

These minds, and more and more minds, continue to arrive on the scene every day, and will do so as long as time and space are still hanging around. I say "hang around" because time and space are hanging around for the time being as the ego's lifeline. This society is not really "secret" in the ego interpretation of the word, but more *discrete*, because the purpose requires that this society of minds remain as uninfluenced as possible by an ego-based thought system.

In other words, maintaining a flamboyant or pompous or grandiose demeanor does not help the society's purpose. In fact, it only sets us back. Instead, we can observe the society's esoteric or hidden nature, a quality of grandeur, which is of God.

The Ego Institution

The fantasies of humankind have become an "institution" to the ego's thought system—a type of confinement that seems to separate itself from its Source. This illusion has developed suffering and pain and death, but humankind has forgotten that it chose this separateness freely, and believes it to be freedom. The illusion expands to believe that because man has the power to be separate, he has the ability to experience anything he wishes. No one can make the impossible real, however, and separation from our Source is impossible; therefore, this remains a dream of fantasy. But it can seem to be real, as do most dreams.

The reawakening I spoke of earlier, our ultimate goal, is actually a release from this confinement and is the willingness to accept the role of being cocreator with God. By becoming completely free of illusion, we experience strength, a thought totally alien to the ego, which believes the opposite. By declaring your own freedom from this prison cell, you release the illusion of separation so it can fade away, and you reassume your place as an integral part of Divine Wholeness, which is your true reality.

The infinite number of members in this society of togetherness and forgiveness may move their focus every so many years, or month to month, or day in and day out. This depends on where the most ego involvement exists, bringing on violence and war, or can be simply due to minor help needed in an area such as the snow-blocked driveway being cleared unexpectedly when you may be rushed.

The violence to which I refer is not limited to physical abuse, but can also take the form of attacks by thoughts and gestures. Some members of this society focus on more volatile areas. But when their level of accomplishment is complete in any one area, or they receive an inner direction to move on, they seem to be easily replaced. Unsurprisingly, given the depth and strength and communication level of the society, this replacement seems to occur automatically, based on the level of thought needed next and the readiness of that member.

No matter how often a member is replaced as his or her task or level of accomplishment is completed, there is always a member positioned in an area until complete healing has taken place. This is not planned or manipulated; it merely shifts as needed. We could say it's a "shift change," so to speak. In other words, someone is always naturally willing to move in who seems to be the most solid resource in helping forgiveness to take its foothold. Or we could say that this member seems to have the appropriate vision to look beyond the errors of the occurrences and is capable of bringing peace to the area, and then wholeness comes forward.

The Procession Line

No doubt as you've been reading this chapter about the secret society, a part of you wishes to chuckle in disbelief, but I expect there's also another part of you that wants to know more. This latter part of you is the same part of me that continues to write of my experiences of never-ending spurts of growth. Our growth occurs in spurts due to ego interference that tries to block it. Ego defense continues.

My own individual position in this society is one step behind many, and one step in front of many others, in a continual procession line of peace. This procession of truth is the interlocking chain of oneness called the process of Atonement. This entails the undoing of errors in our thoughts with corrections leading to total oneness of mind. As long as time exists there will be some ego-based gaps or missing links in its chain.

There will be a point in time, however, when the gaps before us and behind us will be filled, and the chain will be fully linked and welded eternally together as the One-Mind of God. In other words, total reawakening will end the illusion of separation.

This full awakening of humanity will prove that time and space never really existed at all. To "atone" means to undo errors entirely and become whole. But before this can take place there is much more shifting (of illusory belief to perceptions—which are supported by our projected images and some intuition and then to inner divine knowledge) that must occur in all minds. As projections fade away allowing for perception to shift deeper and become pure knowledge, the mind of humanity will heal, and the process is ongoing, everywhere, in every moment.

This shift I speak of is a simple motion from wrong-mindedness to right-mindedness, and from there over the bridge to knowledge. A new way of perceiving the world is happening all over, as the light of truth grows clearer with the Holy Spirit's use of time. This is how real knowledge comes forward in all of us.

Let me say that I do know how many of you must feel. There was a time when, if someone came to me with a story like this, I would have thought they were crazy. But the part of your mind that wants to know more is the real you, and you have been welcomed to this secret society as a brother/sister.

Being that your body is not the real you, I use the word "brother" throughout this book for the purpose of expressing unity and oneness that is beyond any gender connotations of the body, which would only add duality of thought to the picture. Therefore, for you females reading along, please do not be offended when I address you as brother when I really mean brother/sister, or speak of God's "son" or refer to God as "He." These are merely conventional shorthand for *you*—for the Oneness.

Besides, regardless of your level of involvement on this path, you are together along with me and all others as an expression of the wholeness of thought, at-one with God, as His whole Son, or Sonship. If we pause to get hung up on a word, we can credit ego-based interference. It's the meaning behind the word we are seeking, as we share brotherhood as God's Son, and as One Mind—the consciousness behind the body.

The Momentum Is Faith

To keep the momentum moving along within the society, when a new mind or a new group of minds replaces someone who moves on to another area, where needed, they do the same kind of work and follow the same secret tradition based on their readiness. The society consistently involves itself in a certain type of meditation, which varies depending on the level of thought of that person, and which cancels out or reverses much of the negative thought in the world.

This meditation does not focus on bodily requests, such as asking for favors, as though expecting some type of magical spell to be cast. Some prefer prayer to meditation. But either way it replaces the negativity with what is called *forgiving faith*. The prayer or meditation brings forward this "faith" from within, which many like to call "light." Our prayer calls upon the realness in each of us to replace illusory, ego-based perceived notions that were seeded by wrong-minded thoughts.

Think about it. What are your thoughts about all of this at this very moment? To help you feel more comfortable about your answer, I'm sure part of you sees this as perfect sense. This part of you knows as well as I do that we have always wondered and questioned how things work and what is keeping everything held together in this seemingly threatening world.

You and I both know that our spirits work in mysterious ways. This secret society, of which you are a member, is in touch with the answer. The communication link, or Holy Spirit, has already begun to move you toward transcendence, simply by the fact that you are holding this book in your hands. We both realize that you could have tossed this book aside in the very first chapter, but here you are.

We both are also aware that everything happens for a reason, and the Divine Guide, who is our Holy Communicator and Healer, is within all of us. He is shared as One. On some level you have a willingness to know more. To find out how you can know or experience more, ask yourself one question and expect an honest answer: *What should I do next?*

By asking, you have shown you are honestly ready. Next, simply listen for instructions. They will be given to you, and you'll start developing *real vision.*

Chapter 8
Your Real Vision

If there's one thing we all know for sure, it's that no two people in this world are the same. Your perception of the world is much different from mine. We don't even see the same physical world. What we see with the body's eyes is a projection of what we believe.

When something truly urges you to take action, this will be brought forward in you to look at, but not with the eyes that have formed your beliefs. Rather, you will see a vision that sustains your real self. Your instructions will have come forward in your mind. You'll have no doubts.

Why You Believe What You Do

There was a time when I was dreaming about becoming a psychologist, but I never did. It wasn't for me. I remember studying about a research project in which scientists raised a litter of kittens in a room with vertical lines everywhere. When they were grown, the cats were moved to a room with nothing but horizontal lines. They bumped into the walls, ran into objects, and knocked over everything that was horizontal because these confused cats couldn't see anything but vertical.

Everything most of us see and believe in is only there because we believe in it. We have no idea how much we're missing, simply because we don't have a wider frame of reference. We're afraid of expanding or going beyond our frame of reference, which is usually what was passed down to us by previous generations. When we can realize our fears we begin to see things in a whole new way, and then we can move forward. What was always hidden right in front of us can suddenly come to life.

Generation upon generation has piled illusion on top of illusion in our minds, and our true Divinity seems to be buried deep. It's not difficult to reach that area where all truth is revealed. But you must do it. You must go after it with all the sense of realness about yourself you can bring to the table. Call this table your altar if you wish.

What you can do next is to hold firmly in your mind the following single thought, which will help you forgive the world for what "they" did to you. Remember, you must forgive yourself, too. Are you not a part of this world that went along with "their" beliefs?

You must first understand what forgiving really means. By forgiving, I mean you must overlook the ego by looking beyond it, so that you can see true reality. The ego has been blocking the view.

What is true reality, other than the simple truth? Use the words that follow as a meditation or a prayer, whichever way is real thought for you. But as you use these words and as you look beyond the world you see, and the things that upset or frighten you, try to see inner peace as your choice in every action you take. Bring these words into your consciousness, because whether you realize it or not, they are already in your consciousness behind the dream. You must bring this idea through the fog and forward in your mind, so that the idea itself reflects in your projected image. Here are the words; now bring the whole idea to you.

I am as God created me.
(Allow it to sink in.)

This is the thought you must revere deeply. It is simple, just the way it should be. From time to time, repeat this statement to yourself. The meaning behind the words is what you're after. The meaning is deeply rooted and wholly known by all members in the society of "conscious understanding," and is the answer to the illusion you have made on your own. By being a part of these words, you are seeing yourself as true, and you become a model for those who need your help. All untruths will disappear, and dreams of the past will peacefully fade away.

Knowledge Is Not Personal

As you contemplate the past and wonder how our minds could ever have made the ego, you will find that you really cannot answer to the past, only because it no longer exists. You can't ask a question to something that is not present and expect an answer. Others will offer answers for the past in an effort to try and help you out, but that's why we're all in this predicament of an ego-based thought system.

We've all heard it said before and perhaps even said it ourselves: "History would not exist if the same errors were not being repeated over and over in the present." But we seem to take pride in our history and often admire what ancient family members "once said." Knowledge of anything is not a personal issue and should not be understood as so. What I mean is that with knowledge, there is nothing we have to understand, because knowledge is what it is, which is beyond understanding.

Allow me to offer an example, which may seem ridiculous to you— but at least it is simple. Let's say you and I are standing outdoors in the rain while having a conversation that could take a while. Is there anything we should understand about the knowledge we both have as to why we are getting wet, and also why we should take cover to avoid further soaking? No. Due to our common sense, this is automatically understood. But if there were only heavy cloud cover, thunder, and a threat of rain, we might also know it's a good idea to take our conversation under a roof because we have a perception of getting rained on. It may not rain, and our understanding of the possibility of a rain shower did bring us indoors, but it's not necessarily what kept us dry. What did keep us dry was the knowledge that a downpour of rain for its intended purpose would certainly have a "drenching result." We know water is wet and we understand we must take cover from a possible rain shower.

We've all made an ego, or a self, that gives us the image we walk around with, which is seemingly subject to variation because it's unstable. If that's not enough to keep history in its place, we continue to make an ego for everyone else we look at with the body's eyes. *Your image of them* is how you think you understand them to be. How these images interact is a process that changes, because images are not made by God, who is unchangeable. We are a mind within a mind. A mind is not an image.

We must realize that the change we see does occur when we interact in the mind, and the result is projected as a physical appearance. Thinking about another ego is as effective in changing your perception as is physical interaction. This tells us that the ego is surely an idea that we manufactured in our minds. It certainly is not knowledge.

Here's another example. Think of the ways you have viewed another individual when you were filled with jealousy, or guilt, or fear. Your own state of mind at these times proves how that ego was made. Can this show you an excellent portrayal of how the first human, Adam, was made by a guilty and confused separated mind?

These images of man surely are not of man's knowledge, but are only a perception based on projections of an inner feeling. In other words, your projections of another person stem from a perception you have made, and it is not who that person truly is. Do you find this frightening? Or does it give you a sense of direction now?

If we're going to continue to be frightened, and uncertain in life, why is it surprising that it was the same fearful way in the past? Our minds do not need to operate this way, and they're not supposed to.

Chapter 9
The Mission

One winter comes to my mind, when I traveled with my regular group of golf buddies to a golf resort near the Florida Everglades, where the mission at hand was nothing but serious golf vacationing. The seriousness of each shot by each golfer made for the memories that each of us still holds.

At that time of the year the golf course was populated by water moccasins, an aggressive and deadly snake. The groundskeeper posted warning signs near marshy areas that said, "If you see a baby snake, Mama is close by." The protection of Mama here is a good example of the love that nature possesses for its offspring. But think about this. Don't we instinctively protect our egos this way—protect our pride?

What about our so-called loves, charities, and of course our material possessions? Belief in something is a function of the ego within us all, a lesson given shortly after the first tick of time when humankind fell to guilt by separation. As long as the origin of "who you are" remains open to question, you are regarding your beliefs from an ego-based viewpoint.

What I have to say next may not seem very positive at first, but please absorb the thought while leaving room for further contemplation. When *knowledge* is all there is, any beliefs you may have are meaningless. A belief is open to question, and where questions sit so does doubt in the seat adjacent. A belief is a way of perceiving something as the loftiest idea the ego can come up with. Perception always leaves room for interpretation and judgment. If you have considered this closely, it has given you a glimpse at the ego not being who you truly are. Let's face it, an ego can have beliefs, but can never "know for certain." In fact, it has no knowledge at all.

This shows us that the losses we "perceive to have" can only be of the ego. We see this as painful, and we rage over our losses as misfortunes. Consider a small child found playing with something potentially dangerous, such as a knife or scissors. The baby doesn't see it as a dangerous object while having fun and may scream in a tantrum if you take the object away. But it is your responsibility to remove the foreseeable harm. In this sense we are still a child when we get upset about particular losses. Am I saying these losses are for our own good? I'll let you put that together as we move on.

Try to see that we have no sense of our real self and its preservation, and usually decide that we need what hurts us most. We've been afraid for no reason at all of our own true potential, which is who we truly are. This is why I urge you to focus on the thought:

I am as God created me.

Forgiving Grace

I didn't realize it at the time, but later would discover that the deeper I would dive into *A Course in Miracles* and its series of abstractions, a part of me had long ago already decided to be in union with the secret society of "nonjudgment." By cooperating without my ego in particular efforts, I was seeing myself as helpful and harmless, which are attributes that must work together. But the effort was actually *effortless*.

This is the part in all of us that knows what we want, instead of wishful thinking, and also is that real and true aspect in us that completes our real vision. This is wholeness in action. It's the part of you that says, "There's got to be more to this world. I know there's a better way." It is also the part of you that *knows* you've not been truly honest with yourself, instead of only believing so.

This is okay, because our attitudes are ego based and conflicting. So if you can overlook this by looking beyond this ego interference, you have then forgiven yourself. See how easy it is to forgive? This ego-based interaction inside us will always be a part of us to deal with, for as long as we are here on Earth occupying a body. But this is okay, too, as long as you know which aspect of you is truly in charge.

The mission of the secret society involves understanding this, and recognizing automatically when the ego tries to enact its antics. You can learn very simply to put the illusions of the ego in its place with your real self when it attempts corruption. This can be achieved by being patient, and knowing that the ego is only trying to prove that it has a reality. So be kind to yourself by telling yourself that you know better. This knowledge in you is what is called *forgiving grace*. It's the light in you that shines regardless of any ego-based cloud cover.

You can only be truly charitable if you have a real and never-ending sense of abundance. This, you do indeed have. Forgiving Light is the truth in you that is constantly flowing, and is why you have unlimited strength. You are abundant and full and whole, because you have a willingness to look beyond beliefs.

As your consciousness becomes aware of itself it will realize this abundance, which you know to be the truth in every aspect of who you are. By refusing to know yourself, panic sets in as you frantically seek a substitute. This would be the ego, and terror pursues you when you realize you can never replace the eternal, and fear seizes you when you experience the guilt for trying to replace what is forever your true colors.

You must keep in mind that this idea you have of being separate and alone is just that: a thought. But it is a false idea that makes more unreal thoughts. What is an example of an unreal thought? That your true potential relies on your body. This is a nothing idea. The falsities you live by stem from this one unreal thought.

The New Birth

The truth in us as a whole has fallen asleep and is having a dream of separate wholes, with each one having a separate meaning. People everywhere are beginning to rub their eyes and yawn, however, as we slowly move toward reawakening. The world is full of hate and selfishness and greed. But on the other hand, there is more love sprouting up and spreading everywhere than ever before.

It's as though we are seeing the two exact opposites with very little gap between, soon to merge together as one. This is a sign that truth will soon be seen and shine through the cloud cover that has been obscuring our minds. When I grew up in the 1960s, the adults looked at the Beatles, and rock 'n' roll music in general, as a threat of some kind. Many of the adults were seeing the youth as moving forward with change. Today we are the adults who have seen and experienced love being extended as a result of music. The examples are everywhere. Reality is in the process of giving birth to reality, and oneness of mind is the umbilical cord.

Have you ever been dreaming something that is frightening or upsetting, when a part of you realizes it's only a dream? Sure you have. This dreaming part of humanity is realizing a new birth, and as a whole it is a *shift* toward total realization of our unity, as being of the One Mind of God. We are not separate, and the Holy Spirit is using time for the healing process. This is happening now, all around us. At times it may seem painful, but you are here for the purpose of helping everyone to eventually breathe eternal air.

If you are serious about helping, even if it's only helping yourself for now—which is a great start—you must see that a dreaming mind can fathom whatever it wishes, but cannot make itself real. It can make entire worlds that run by completely different laws, but when the mind wakes up it finds that reality has not changed.

People live in fear, and as this awakening progresses, that same fear will have to be released. If it is not, the birth will be chaotic and traumatic. Your place is peace, and your purpose is forgiveness at whatever level it might be. But there is much we must learn about forgiveness. Its basic principle is to clearly "overlook the ego by looking beyond it." If you can remember this principle, forgiveness will become easy for you to understand and to accept.

To overlook is to give of yourself, but we've been taught by the world that to overlook means to be cautious. Do you see how backward and self-defeating the ego is? Let's now shift forward to the next, important part of this book, so you can begin to turn this around.

PART II
THE SHIFT THROUGH TIME

Chapter 10
Your Shift to Abundance

The ego tries to taint your own true colors into believing you'll have to do without; you make yourself feel lacking. But when you overlook an ego antic for the nothingness it is, you are forgiving yourself, or whoever else has tried to fool you.

"Overlooking," and thereby forgiving, doesn't mean you should be afraid to give a firm "no" to a situation or to request that someone simply pardon you from any further involvement with them because the relationship is not right for you. There may seem to be a sacrifice involved, but turning away from a negative involvement is not a sacrifice. When you do feel that you have sacrificed, this is intended by the ego to suggest that you are rightfully owed, or due something better, and can therefore sacrifice now in order to get more later; for example, giving up a TV show, or going to bed an hour later, or rising for the day an hour earlier.

The ego's golden rule seems to be "Give now in order to get later." This "giving" or "giving up" is usually compared in relation to other egos. The ego will also try to fool you and come in the back door by "giving" so that it may receive "Divine" favors, even though it has no interest in you living Divinely. The ego has a preoccupation with scarcity thoughts that keep it thinking it might be missing out on something.

Self-Esteem Is Not Required

Our "secret society" is that of real minds and has no needs at all, which includes not having to prove anything or feel we're "missing out" on something. The ego perceives other egos as being real, and uses this perception to try to convince itself it is real too. In contrast, the society of *truth and abundance* does not require self-esteem. This may seem at first to be an arrogant statement. In ego terms, however, "self-esteem" means nothing more than fooling yourself, or "esteeming" yourself, into believing you are something you're not—and doing so with a convincing wrong-mind.

The real you does not need to be "esteemed." If you are praising yourself, then you are judging yourself, but what is real requires no judging. Remember, the ego is nothing more than a fantasy "maker," or dream of what you wish to be. You think that you must judge this *wish* in order to get where you will never go. This is so because it's not what you truly *want*.

Keep in mind, when I speak of the ego, I am not speaking of something possessed only by others. So when you shake your head in disgust, it is toward an aspect in yourself that has gotten out of control. The good news is that the ego is not real, but it does indeed seem to have us all fooled.

We've all been taught to give, and the ego feels safe in giving when it's by comparisons. The ego cannot understand equality, and true charity is impossible. The ego will never be abundant because it is always wanting more; therefore, it can never give out of abundance. The ego may feel abundant at times, but only briefly due to its constant worry about lacking. Please ask yourself this question honestly: Does it make you feel good to give?

This is how the concept of "getting" has come to life in the ego's thought system. Don't get me wrong here; you should feel complete when you give, as long as you realize where this "good" feeling is coming from. When the good becomes your true knowledge, and you are aware you are giving because that's what is in your heart, then truth is felt throughout and extends to whomever you're giving. Their truth will *know* the truth in you. By contrast are not egos aware of each other when ulterior motives are involved?

In the chapters ahead, you'll read about situations where, through the secret society, we have recognized and discovered one another when help was needed. Many times the giver was not even aware that the receiver had actually received guidance or help.

We said in my first book, *The Master of Everything*, that "giving and receiving are different aspects of the same thought," and there is no lacking in between, because there's no gap. This is how your own feelings of lack can comfortably shift over to abundance: mind to mind, or perhaps better phrased, *mind within mind*. It's that simple. It's all about darkness being drawn to the light.

Striving to Get

The ego is always striving. Think about our appetites of any kind. These are bodily "getting" mechanisms, representing the ego's need to acknowledge to itself that it surely has its needs. The real you will see that the body gets nutrition, along with some pleasure in doing so. But the ego will take its striving for food to its own level, where it's never satisfied.

The appetite for food is a good example of a mechanism of getting, in order to satisfy a need called hunger. It goes much further when the ego says, "Okay, I ate a healthy meal; now give me that sugar!" The ego regards the body as its temple, trying to satisfy itself through the body.

The ego believes it originated out of thin air, or from "dust," a kind of magic it wishes to believe is a miracle and that is on its own, making its own way in the world. It believes that *dust* is where it shall return. A frightening belief, wouldn't you agree? This is a confused and fearful state, where the ego needs other egos to help it with its own unique identification. The ego assembles religiously with other egos to give praise to this kind of magic, which it tries to understand, and to further its beliefs in something waiting "out there" to grant salvation. But the ego struggles over what it actually needs saving from—its own existence. So the fear continues.

The ego is always striving to gain your spirit's attention and to prove an existence of its own. But what the ego will never understand is that spirit is the knowledge you possess, and your knowledge of *what* and *who* you are is unaware of the ego. Only you as an ego can be aware of the ego. When we were kids, didn't we say, "It takes one to know one?"

The real you in its wholeness cannot conceive of an ego at all. The ego believes that it can be rejected by something greater than itself if it doesn't live up to certain standards. This is why self-esteem is delusional, but strived for by the ego. Remember, the ego is not intentionally or naturally bad; it's just extremely erroneous in its thought system.

God's Creation, of course, is not erroneous, but it is certainly real, and therefore has no need to make myths. While there have been creative efforts to make mythology, whatever the ego makes is not a creation. These myths are entirely of a perception that is uncertain in form, featuring a system of good-versus-evil, in which the "good" side of the form is not intended to be fearful.

Myths and magic are closely tied together, since myths are usually used to explain body (ego) origins, and magic usually relates to the powers the ego wishes to believe it came from. Mythological systems usually include some account of the creation and associate it with a particular form of magic. The so-called battle for survival is only the ego's struggle to perceive itself and its interpretation of its own beginning. The beginning is usually associated with physical birth, because it's difficult to maintain that the ego existed before that point in time.

The more religiously ego-oriented may believe that the soul existed before and will continue to exist after a temporary lapse into ego life on Earth. Some even believe that the soul might be punished for this lapse, such as the belief in a purgatory. St. Augustine built up the idea from St. Paul that all souls are born into this world with original sin, and a few religions then decided that baptism would cleanse this sin away. Salvation does not apply to true spirit, however. Why? Because your true spirit, that true peace and joy about you, is one with God. Who could possibly have the job of saving God?

The Ego Will Tire Itself Out

If knowledge is spirit, and of course this would mean that spirit knows all there is to know about you, which is your oneness with God, then how can any aspect of knowledge be saved, and saved from what? I realize this was discussed earlier. But this time try to study that question for a moment or so, and go ahead and listen to the ego's input. Let the ego tell you of all the things you need saving from. It will tire itself out trying to prove to you all the things you should be fearful of or stand guard against.

Okay, now that you've had your little consultation from the ego, which you made, let's move on. What we're trying to understand is really quite simple. You have an inner knowledge that tells you that you are *not* your ego. This is your spirit. And then there is a part of you that can't make heads or tails of your spirit, and never will. This is your ego.

Bear with me now. Let's face it, when you're not being yourself, don't you truly know about this little charade you've made up? Is it the ego that senses your untruthful game being played? How could it be, when the ego is not real? The ego can sense nothing, but it can reside in fantasy and fear. It fears losing its untruthful identity. It is the real you that has the knowledge of the entire charade, so simply let it go by letting the truth in you be shown.

With this realized, now you can see salvation as nothing more than accepting this knowledge. In this sense you are saved, or we can say "born again." Look at this deeply and see who you are. You have the ability to operate from right-mindedness by choice and to quickly spot ego interference.

This is not to be confused with the One-mindedness of the Holy Spirit, our ultimate state once full Atonement is achieved. But total right-mindedness must be achieved before One-mindedness can be restored. I use the word "restored" here because isn't this your true state of mind behind the dream of "judgment and separation?"

We actually do possess One-mindedness now, but the ego is obscuring our vision, some of us more or less obscured to the Light. Our right-mind leads us to the next step automatically, because right-minded perception moves in a direction that leaves attack behind, and this is a state where wholeness will find us. This will completely obliterate the ego and its wrong-mindedness, with the Holy Spirit's use of time. The ego cannot survive without judging itself, let alone other egos. Sooner or later it will have no choice but to fade away into the dust it says it came from. Total nothingness.

Your Immortality

With ego on the sidelines and your spirit in control, the mind has only one direction in which it can proceed. It is the right-mind's direction that will be automatic, because now it knows it cannot be dictated to by the ego's thought system. Its only choice is one way. You may experience this when you make a decision on a matter without hesitation or doubt or questions, and you proceed to knowingly make the right turn.

It cannot be emphasized too often that correcting perception is merely a temporary fix. It's necessary only because our mis-perceptions are a block to knowledge, while accurate perception gets us there via a route through the right-mind. It's a stairway up, through, and above the fog. The higher the steps take you, the less fog there is obscuring the way. The whole value of right-minded perception rests in the inevitable realization that all perception is unnecessary. This removes the obstruction entirely. You may ask how this is possible, as you appear to be living in this world. This is a reasonable question.

You can understand this more clearly if I ask you a simple question: Who is the "you" who is living in this world? You may answer by saying,

"I am Tom," and you may add a last name or a job description. But in reality you are thought, and the real nature of thought is spirit. Spirit is immortal, and immortality is a constant state that has no opposite. It is as true now as it ever was or ever will be. This is why my friend Tom admits that he forever lives, regardless of the image we have of him.

Chapter 11
That Place of Zero Ego Involvement

"A place of supreme happiness, beyond the sky; the abode of God, where the angels and the souls of those who have been granted salvation abide." This is a definition of Heaven that's been passed along to us by past generations for thousands of years. This also paraphrases the standard dictionary description of our eternal resting place.

There is no doubt in my right-mind that this description was made by man so that the good in all of humanity might freely come forward. However, with our total right-mindedness, let's take this well-intended set of promising words that project an image of Heaven and go much deeper—without the body pictured—and see that the knowledge within you is the oxygen the Kingdom of Heaven gives you to breathe. Once you have deeply thought this over, let's use real vision to see the angels everywhere in our lives.

Heaven Is Yours

We've all heard it said: "May the Kingdom of Heaven be yours." Most of us have never really considered what this means, other than picturing Heaven as some location far away. The phrase suggests that someplace outside of us will welcome us at some point, or invite us in as a just reward. We may picture streets paved in gold somewhere beyond all the galaxies, or a puffy pink cloud upon which we ride, or any of the many other mythical illustrations that promote the supernatural.

Instead, let's take the fantasy out of the picture and understand that the Kingdom of Heaven is you, because it is within you. The Kingdom is you because you are what God created. There is nothing else but you. There is nothing else it could be, because this is the whole message of the Atonement. Heaven is that essence of our minds wholly linked together and then welded by our Guide, the Holy Spirit, with His effortless communication, until all minds are gapless.

You, as the Kingdom, have created a spirit, and regardless of the ego you have not stopped creating. It is that spirit of who you are that has an interest in this book you read now. It is that spirit that freely interprets my words for how they pertain to you, without dissecting the meaning of each word. It's that acknowledgment of being more, which you inwardly feel you can be when you involve yourself with a willingness to forgive.

You and your ego will never be cocreators, but your spirit and your Creator will always be creating together, and this is Heaven. You are creating every time you experience the extension of joy, which is a direct result of peace, and each is a result of Love.

But the ego in each of us regards any activity of our spirits, and the spirit itself, as the enemy, and each ego has its own battle plan. Given the number of egos, or individuals, on this planet, it's no surprise there is so much chaos, confusion, greed, lying, and war. This is the work of the billions of individual battle plans in action. In our separateness, what we fight we only get more of.

The ego must have you on its side, believing in separation, in order for it to remain separate, and to continue to teach its separate ways for the generations to follow. But the ego is losing ground with time as its enemy, and as it slowly but surely fades, it continues to offer a supposed Heavenly reward for maintaining the belief of separation. The ego tries to make you feel arrogant when you accept your oneness with God. The ego insists that God is somewhere outside of you, but always at your side. It will raise an argument if you don't believe so, and will feel just in its attack.

The ego's argument is that the "Gates of Heaven" wait for you. It emphasizes the "gate" to Heaven as some sort of blockade, or an approved entrance area where only those who have "earned the right" may enter. It also stresses that you must first be questioned by the "Gatekeeper" and pass that test before being admitted to your reserved space.

Any offer the ego has for you is always temporary, and it will tell you that "this is what life is all about." However, spirit can give you a sense of permanence and unshakable being through the air it breathes called knowledge. No one who has ever experienced this knowledge from within can ever again trust or believe the ego when it tries to communicate.

When you identify with the ego, it must mean that you are not certain of your unified oneness with God. It means, as well, that you have questions about whether or not you do have a Creator. But don't worry; this thought has crossed all our minds, thanks to the ego. This is only your own separateness being afraid to heal.

Your Free Will Guides You

There is not a force in all of eternity that is strong enough or worthy enough to guide you, except for your own true free will. In this free will of yours is the Spirit of God, and in the Holy Spirit's giving this free will to you, all giving and receiving will remain yours. "Ask and you shall receive" is both true and necessary so you may have the resources available to give.

Jesus, the man, who extended this idea to us as our elder brother and leader of the Atonement process, has asked us to stay mindful of the Oneness, our Divinity, which the Atonement stands for. The spirit of Jesus, through the Christ-Mind we all share, stands at the end as the final welded link in the chain, where completion is guaranteed. We can say the Christ-Mind is the whole Sonship personalized, onto which you may project the image that suits you. For example, in a casual conversation I had, someone used the idea that Christ can be seen as the "brain," so to speak, that operates God's Whole Son, or Sonship. With this understanding we can see the Sonship as our relationship with Oneness.

Full Atonement within this relationship, or the end of time, is where we will all appear as Christ. This will be the Final Judgment, but rather than a meting out of punishment, as the ego sees it, this is when all the love we could have will exist without conflict, when we are free of all illusion, and reality will be the vision. Fantasy will no longer have an attraction, and not really an event "in time."

How, in the realm of One-mindedness, can a single conflict exist? This is what is really meant by the statement "Thou shalt have no other gods," because there are none. The Holy Spirit has intended for us to use this wonderful statement as a devotion to Truth, rather than a demand. But over the generations the ego has interpreted this as a direct order or a rule for obedience called a "commandment." It's as though the ego has worked diligently toward teaching us that we see God as a commander.

The Decision to Surrender

Let's take a quick breather here, because we've been going deep, and deeper still we need to go. For the moment, just suppose you made the decision to surrender every idea you've ever had that opposes knowledge, by releasing this wrong-mindedness and allowing the Holy Spirit to deal with it for you. If you let go of it all now, what do you think would happen?

We all hold within us a mind full of illusory thoughts that feed our fears. This prevents us from seeing the sights arranged by our Guide, who roams the separated mind, with oneness as His goal.

When I say that "you" must surrender these untruths, I mean your true essence behind the frame that is your body. The "you" I'm writing about is the abstractness beyond the fear that the frame holds—the tapestry itself that has nothing to do with flesh and bones. This is the Christ in you that others sense when you walk into a room. It's the *Jewel* about you.

Let's take another deep dive within, away from the body, by answering a few questions that may help you transcend. Try to put all physical thoughts aside, or ask the Holy Spirit to temporarily hold onto them for you, leaving you in touch only with that inner essence that is you. But if you cannot put all thoughts aside at this time, that's okay; read on regardless, because the message will sink in.

Think of that split instant when you first hear that wood hen hammering away as it hollows out an oak tree, the sound echoing while you are slowly walking through a forest. In that instant, the flash of no-time, where is the place in your mind that first registers this bliss? Or in the moment you sight a shooting star arc across a velvety night sky, where is the awe-inspiring vision resting while your breath is taken away? How about the feeling of cradling a newborn baby in your arms, and when she smiles and gurgles, where is the connecting point that inspires the joyful, peaceful smile on your face?

The place that holds these instants of sensation before your brain is triggered is your true Home. This is the Kingdom of Heaven within you. In that instant, time doesn't exist and is where you live ego-free. No ego involvement can dare think about penetrating, because time is not available in order to birth a single thought. Here is where you see God.

Chapter 12
To Have and to Be

The ego has often asked us to "Be careful what we wish for," and it has surely been correct. When you wish for something, at best you will experience only fantasy, nothing real. The ego also tells us that "All good things must end." Being that the ego in us sees fantasy as real and good, it is correct again, in the fact that it is temporary itself. It also advises us to "Enjoy it while it lasts."

What we wish for is a temporary fix, but when we truly *want* something, you can count on reality being involved. To *want* is to make a demand for something that is a necessary ingredient to complete your true free will. The Holy Spirit will arrange that you do indeed easily receive what you want. He will take your demand seriously. This is not an arrogant stance, but wishful thinking is.

Taking Inventory

You must be willing to take an inventory of all your doubts and fears and carefully look at them. Then truly decide what it is you want. The Holy Spirit asks that you hide nothing from Him, but in reality, you can't. He is the aspect of your mind that ensures that all that is real, and all that is intended to be real, arrives on the scene. If you can begin to look at your doubts and fears, you will see with real vision the nothingness they come from. You will have taken the first step toward preparing your mind for success. The peaceful path will begin leading you to true reality, or what we call the real world.

The Holy Spirit will not only make sure you have what you need, but He trusts you in your "wanting" of it, and you will have it. He wants to work together with you, and once you're willing, your participation in this secret society will help other minds to begin seeing the Guiding Aspect of their own mind. How do you participate?

You may not even realize the effects you have on other minds, just as others have not realized their effects on your mind, and both benefit from this learning. But don't dwell on this or try to analyze or dissect it. Simply leave this method of operation up to the Holy Spirit, while He communicates through your own willingness in linking your knowledge to others. What you *can* do is to remember that your brother is that true essence beyond the frame you see as a body. He is your brother, who shares the unseparated mind as the Son of God. This is where giving and receiving become aspects of the same thought within the same whole mind. This is true Divinity.

In your own mind will come a point of declaration of independence from the ego, and a declaration of dependence to your own free will. This free will of yours may seem to be selfish, at least for a moment, until you see that this is only the ego's belief. But if it is a true free will, given to you by God in the Creation, where giving and receiving are the same, then how can it be selfish when it is shared with God? Your declaration of dependence to your free will tells yourself the ego doesn't exist, and for a while you may experience a part of you being afraid. But don't worry too much over this fear, because it's only the ego crying the blues.

Having What You Want

The ego tries to teach us that "to have" and "to be" are different. This is not so according to the Holy Spirit's interpretation, and from your right-mind He is constantly inspiring you and reinforcing the fact that you do indeed "have" and "are" everything that exists. How can our Divinity be whole without you?

Remember, the ego wishes to tell you that "to have" is a "getting" result due to a lack of something. But the Universal Inspiration teaches that we are the Kingdom of Heaven, because you and I are God's Creation. With that, you and I both "have" and "are" the kingdom, and lack nothing.

Any doubting thoughts you have about this come from the ego, because whatever is questionable is due to lack of wholeness, which is separateness. This is why seeing yourself as a body raises questions. You raise doubt about yourself by placing too much emphasis on the body, but to relinquish this habit can be easy to do. For instance, when you look in the mirror first thing in the morning, simply ask yourself, "Who is this looking in the mirror?"

Look again and see if you notice the real you, the *overseer* or the *spectator* of this messy-haired reflection, and watch the gloom fade away. Then notice that the real Overseer is with you to guide you through your day. Use this little trick on seemingly miserable mornings and watch your true essence shine. Sure, you may notice dark circles under your eyes, but you will also be quick to recognize that you need more rest and less stress in your life—a right-minded goal to lead you away from ego-based thinking. As my good friend Zig Ziglar once said, "Get rid of stinking thinking." Then a calmness will move in and take over because you'll know something magnificent is definitely beyond your body.

This calmness of being is what populates God's kingdom. A bit further ahead, you will learn how this calmness connects and how it is shared. It then becomes a vision of oneness and wholeness, and is a situation the ego can never rule over. This makes the ego desperate because it literally faces invincible odds, whether asleep or awakened to reality. The ego is aware the body has its end, but you are eternal.

This cannot be explained completely by words, because the ego made words, and it likes to dissect those words for its own interpretation. Rather, please see my words as a traffic sign, interpreted by the Holy Spirit in you, and in me while I am writing them. He will give these words to you in a fashion He sees as suitable, based on your needs and readiness to receive them.

When you see a stop sign while driving your car, you don't get out of your car to get a closer look or dissect the word's meaning. You automatically know what it means and act accordingly. Similarly, please allow the words I have chosen, which are right for me, to find automatic acceptance in a way that is right for you. Then you may begin to know your own true self beyond the "bad hair" or "no hair" image you see in the mirror—and thus travel on a path that best suits you because it's what you *want*, and not what is wished for by the ego.

This place that holds what you *want* is where you must see the world from. So when you hear the ego in you saying something like "You must sacrifice this in order to get that, so when your time has come God may take you with Him," you can stop and smile. You will truthfully be able to say to yourself, "I've always been with God, and will eternally be." Don't allow the ego to convince you that sacrifice is a "getting" mechanism. Sacrifice is not an ingredient in the Holy Spirit's recipe for your success.

Chapter 13
Is Space the Divider?

Everything we see in this world has been assigned a name, which becomes its identity. Take the clock, for example. It is a timepiece that keeps us organized into days, months, years, and a lifetime. Then there are individuals, such as myself, Jim, and I am a writer, formerly a financial advisor, and now also a convicted felon, as well as a father, grandfather, ex-husband, son, brother, and friend. The world has its choice in giving me an identification tag that suits its purpose at the particular time it brings me to mind. The projection of others determines this.

For eons, humanity has used names to carve out sections from unity or oneness. A separate unit is then the effect, divided or split apart by space. This space, which is also given a name, is the divider that causes the appearance of separate occurrences in terms of place and time, where all bodies are greeted by name.

As important as space is in this task, we still see it as nothing; yet we believe we are separate in many ways. How can space be nothing, if it separates who we are and is responsible for our separate identities? Or—does it really divide us? But without space, how could our bodies ever appear to exist, let alone survive? Isn't there space even between the heart and lungs?

Can it be this space is the part of the unity that holds the body together? Is that infinite and vast nothingness that allows music to exist a space that acts like some sort of glue? If space is nothingness, then "nothing" must be what makes our bodies seem to be alive. How could we walk, run, wave our hand, or speak, just to mention a few, without the help of space?

How would you notice those dark circles under your eyes when you look in the mirror on a gloomy morning if there were no space? Where would gloom come from? We see this space as setting off all things from one another, which is the means by which the world develops a perception of how things appear to not only be, but operate as well.

No Space? How Odd!

A world without space is difficult to comprehend. Why? Because the ego will automatically step in and tell you something like, "Without space, all you would see is endless bodies attached to one another—a chaotic mess, with mass confusion. It's ridiculous to even suggest such a situation." This, of course, makes no sense—my point being that the ego makes no sense, which is why it cannot begin to understand wholeness. The ego cannot visualize anything without bodies somehow being involved, nor can it tolerate even the thought of unity unless it's used for gain.

Regardless of the ego's thought structure, however, take away the body and physical matter, and what we have is simply space. Or does space really exist if there's no physical presence to witness it? Your ego may now be giving this thought a good effort—accompanied by some frustration, wishing I would move on or clarify further meaning. My point is this: While we're here in the dream of separate bodies, and separate lives, and separate wills and freedoms, we interact through the use of space. We made this space by projecting it into the dream to hide ourselves from one question. It is an in-depth question that we just can't seem to answer and are really afraid of its truthful antidote to our problems.

Here it is: What really is beyond these names the world uses to become a part of a series of events, set by these individual wills of things, of bodies held apart by space and holding bits of mind-thought as an awareness? Let's dive deeper to find the answer.

Being Tuned In

The body's own brain dreams up these names, establishing a perception as we wish it to be. This way we may secure our own separateness from one another. Any nameless things are always given a name, which also "gives" them a reality.

Once something is named, it of course must then have a meaning, and from that point is considered to be meaningful. This becomes an effect without a true cause, thus making a consequence for itself. This puts humans in charge of their own *cause and effect,* which is why there is so much chaos in the world we see with our body's eyes.

This is the method by which the world's reality is made, purposefully setting this "reality" against truth. This is not creation. The reality the world thinks it is aware of sees wholeness as its enemy. It conceives of little things and looks up to them. It fears anything too magnificent. When something comes around that lacks this divider called space, and has a sensation of unity or a vision that sees differently, the ego perceives a threat that the world must overcome. We must learn to deny this type of conflict.

I have held back on identifying the name of the secret society I've already introduced. It is a garden of sprouting minds that sees no space, therefore overlooking bodies by looking beyond them when someone has a need to be met. The vision remains a natural direction for the mind to channel its perceptions into right-minded alertness.

Within time, and *time* being exactly what the Holy Spirit uses for His Teaching, you will find yourself a member of what we call "the Little Garden Society." We use the word "Little" to suggest a no-threat image, but in its grandeur a physical size has no meaning. This is where you will come to understand what real learning means to the physical world.

The goal within the Little Garden Society is to achieve communication so that concepts can be meaningfully shared. The world doesn't doubt that when something is not given a name it must not exist.

In the Garden this is understood, and this society surely is seen by the ego of the world as nonexistent. To question what the world ego may say to be real is seen as madness, and to accept it without qualms is the proof of sanity to the ego. It's a phase of learning that everyone who comes along in the world seemingly must go through.

But there is part of every individual that conceptually has, at one time or another, come face to face with an awareness that there is "something more" to this world. This is your welcome to the Little Garden Society. Some tap into it and others don't. Of the ones who do, some are more tapped in than others—a level of being "tuned in," if you will.

The part of you that does tap in is the part of you that exposes the ego for the nothingness it is, and its premise that is questionable and has doubtful results. In other words, the part of you tapped into the Garden is the part of you that wants to read the remainder of this book with an open mind. This is the part of you that questions the world's causes, which make its own effects. Are you ready to move forward and discover a new type of perception that will override your doubt?

This is where you can begin to see reality, rather than allowing a single name to dictate its meaning. All the arbitrary names the world has placed on everything can be withdrawn and seen in the light of true reality.

Chapter 14
The Name You Choose For Reality

Can we, as physical bodies, truly say that we made a world? Hardly. But illusions that have put together this world? Yes! However, the truth in this world and of Heaven is beyond having a nametag.

When we call on another individual, most likely it's to the body by using his or her given name, and the perceived notions that make the images we place effort into giving that person. His or her true identity is hidden and separated by space from our beliefs in this individual. The body makes a response based on what we call a person, and his mind consents to the name we assign. In this, an individual's unity is twice denied, because we perceive that individual as separate from ourselves, and he or she accepts this separateness.

The Little Garden Society is able to go beyond all names the world uses as labels. This society of minds can forget what these names represent, forever, and willingly takes on a teaching function. We're all teachers at some level. We must use the names assigned by the world while we're here, as long as we don't allow them to deceive us. These names are merely a means for communication in ways the world may understand, when using the body to communicate. It's understandable that we use some illusion much of the time in order to live in a world of illusion. But we must also recognize that the means is not the unity where true communication can be found.

But the unity of mind does rest in the fact that we do communicate with one another around the world from our unconscious, and are consciously aware we do so, but may not be consciously aware of the timing of this true communication. Keep in mind that the unconscious I speak of here is the same as the consciousness you are from behind the dream. The dream of separation itself, where you see, hear, and touch physical bodies, is the consciousness that is the ego's domain. Just try to understand that *unconsciousness* in this text does not imply physical sleep or coma.

The timing of the giving and receiving of this type of communication is closely monitored by the Holy Spirit. As I have already mentioned, some minds are more receptive than others, and at any given time, your own state of readiness and willingness may be deeper.

Naming Things

As you continue to read, a foundation is being prepared so you can easily come forward in your mind to the concepts described. For now, consider this: Think of a Divine word that represents your belief system, and take away the manmade letters of the word, leaving only empty space. How, then, do you understand or communicate the word? What is its meaning to you?

A Divine word or name, such as God, was given to us by man. Since God did not create the alphabet or assign itself this name, this word that describes your creation does indeed exist without letters. It is the One Identity that does not have to be spoken or pronounced in order to communicate. It is the One Acknowledgment of all that is true, regardless of the appearance or image of letters in any given language. But if we must physically express our Creator, it is simply convenient for much of the world to say "God" or another deity name.

Now take a moment and think of all the names the world has given you about many things—not because you think they are real, but only to show the unreality in terms that still have meaning in the world; that the world thinks it rules. In other words, think of the words that have meaning without the use of their name. For example, can you communicate or relate the meaning of words like *Being* or *Grace* or *Faith* without using their names? How about without the use of your body?

Okay, now I can hear some of you saying that I must be "off my rocker." But I hope I have you using your mind! Use these names if you must, but are they truly your reality? The Holy Spirit uses all of them, but He doesn't forget that Creation has only one name, one meaning, with no letters or space. This name is a Single Source from which all of reality extends.

By all means, go ahead and use all the names the world gives us for your convenience; yet don't forget they share the name of this Source along with you—if, that is, we must think in terms of naming things at all.

The Meanings Are Unified

The names assigned by the world, such as God, Christ, Holy Spirit, Prayer, Therapy, Mind Consciousness, and so many more, have no special patent or copyright held by religions or the psychological community. You are free to use their meanings, or call the Source any name that is comfortable for you. The Oneness of God will not be offended, and you're not being disrespectful. You may ruffle some ego feathers, as the ego will differ and call it sinful to change names around, but that's okay. It's not our goal to suggest or change names. It is the conscious and the unconscious meaning that speaks for what these words stand for, and even what they actually are.

The Oneness of God has not a name consisting of letters with space between them, which were somberly pronounced to the world. No such physical announcement was made. All the names we use, and their meanings, are unified, and all space is filled with the reflection of the truth in them, and from them.

The function of the Little Garden Society is to bring forward in our minds the acceptance of this reflection of truth as the answer to all the external, meaningless nothingness we made, which brings on conflict in the world. Why do we wish to argue over the proper pronunciation of a word, or its meaning, or how it should or should not be used? The answer is: Because the ego lives in, and by, conflict.

But we can make it easy on ourselves, when from the wholeness we are, we just accept the name we choose for all of reality, without being physically obligated to pronounce it. With this, all foolishness of separation and divisions, which is what keeps our vision obscured, disappears.

Take this thought process now and see beyond all names given by the generations of the world. You now have the choice of a vision that is blessed, and with blessings you can give, as you receive them as well. Can you now see in this thought that giving and receiving are one?

In this space in your mind, where letters and words have been removed, is where healing of separation occurs, and is your part in the Atonement. You have forgiven the world because you have looked beyond it.

Chapter 15
Accepting Yourself

I hope you are traveling through this book at a comfortable pace for you, much as you would while driving on the highway on an exciting and overdue vacation—enjoying the landscape as you travel in and out of different states, growing ever more relaxed as you anticipate your destination. Try to see the words and sentences in the chapters of this book as you might view or experience the different roads you take on your trip, all of them for your enjoyment and a feeling of "getting somewhere."

In this chapter, however, I ask that you adjust your speed when necessary as you move along, as though minor roadwork is in progress in the miles ahead, with yellow caution lights for your attention. Please read without interrupting your rhythm, but slowing your speed if you must. The key is to let the real meaning be yours.

What we are about to discuss has even raised caution in my own writing of the section, and the pace of my thought process is adjusted so that important words are not forgotten. My goal is that you have a successful journey, not only throughout the rest of this book, but for your time here on Earth. The area ahead I consider to be delicate, so please bear with me as we move along through this zone. The goal is that we are in the same zone, together.

While continuing on, ask yourself, or think about, what it is that frightens you about this world. Is it the uncertainty of the world, or is it the uncertainty about yourself?

If I were to go around announcing to everyone I run into that my mission is to save the world, wouldn't you agree most others would question my sanity? This is the type of attention the ego strives for. Yet, it is my mission to help the world, and so is it yours. It is the part in all of us that ends all choice.

It is the decision to accept ourselves as God created us. When we give ourselves choices, something to decide, we're telling ourselves that we accept uncertainty of who we are. Why do we doubt who we are? What is it we are so uncertain about? It always seems to be this simple question that haunts us: *What am I?* And, on a deeper level, we often ask: *Why am I here?*

Our Doubts

Any uncertainty we have about ourselves is frightening, as it is not a very secure feeling. Why is this? Because it is self-deception at a magnitude that can hardly be conceived. Deception is always an edgy feeling, let alone the vastness of our own deceiving. To be alive and not know yourself is to believe you don't exist.

Remember, you make this a frightening question when you see yourself as only a body. Think about it. What really is life, except to be yourself? What else but you can be alive? Or, how can anyone else be alive without your existence?

Holding that thought, consider the sounds Mother Nature makes, say, deep in the woods, with no one around to witness the beauty. If there is a babbling brook flowing and trickling over rocks echoing in that wilderness, bouncing off trees, with no human body present, does the brook really speak or sing? Additionally, is the brook really flowing? Finally, is there really a brook?

When you doubt something, as we all do, who is the one doing the doubting? What is it that this "doubter" is doubting? To whom can this doubter raise this question, and who is it within yourself that can answer?

Of course, you might be saying to yourself that you are the doubter, and that it is simply you who is not being your true self. If this is so, then you must be something else. This "something else" becomes the questioner of what things are. Yet he could never be alive unless he knew the answer. If he asks as if he doesn't know, it merely shows he does not want to be the thing he is. He has accepted it because he does truly live, but has judged against it, denied its worth, and decided he doesn't know the only certainty by which he lives. He must exist in order to make such a decision.

Now he becomes uncertain of his life, for what he is has been denied by him. Because of this denial, you—the real you—needs Atonement. This means you need some serious *undoing* of errors in thinking, or what is called wrong-mindedness, because your denial has made no change in what you are.

Your mind has been split from a part that knows, and into many fragments that do not know, the truth. There truly is no doubt you are yourself, and yet you doubt it. But you don't ask what part of you can really doubt yourself. It can only be the true part of you that asks the question, because it asks of the One Who Knows the answer. But believe it or not, only you have the knowledge of this "One."

This may seem confusing, and rightfully so with egoic defensive thinking. The likelihood of getting egoic feedback is the reason I asked that you travel with caution on this stretch of the road. But I can tell you, as I have learned, Atonement is the only remedy to this strange idea of being able to doubt yourself—being unsure of *what* and *who* you really are.

But what is Atonement in this regard? How do we use it as a remedy?

First of all, Atonement is the clearing away of the errors, or the wrong-mindedness, we live by. Then it is the acceptance that this is the path to healing our separate identity.

We Do Have a Mission Here

The healing of our separate identity has always been the universal missing link to the chain of inner connectedness. The separated state has brought about much madness, but anything that separates from its Source will experience loss, chaos, and fear. Is it any wonder that we live in a mad world?

Why are we so passive in the face of this madness, and afraid to show our real selves to this sad belief we've had, that what is questionable or doubtful is true? But only *nothing* can be doubtful, which is what the ego is. Fantasy or illusion is made by separate wishes that are a false idea of reality. At best these wishes can only seem real in time. Therefore, are your wishes what forms your beliefs?

Consider that nothing the world believes is true. I know, that statement may be similar to me asking you to consider the grass being purple. But isn't a belief in anything merely a way to claim what we don't really know?

When you think about it, couldn't we say that a belief is a wannabe truth, made in order to satisfy an uncertainty? Only the ego is uncertain, but it hopes that one day magic will prevail and open the gates to Heaven, where we'll finally find answers. This kind of believing is the ego's lessons that the answers we seek today will be our just reward when we die. By following this lesson, how could we then ever know anything, if we must wait until our death?

To die certainly means "no life," the last I understood it. How could there be knowledge in that mode? This is the vicious cycle you live by until the moment Atonement is accepted and you learn it is impossible to doubt yourself any longer, and to not be aware of what you truly are. Your function is to heal, and think about it—isn't that what we do constantly? Healing in some manner is always taking place. When you accept Atonement you do so from knowledge, not from a belief. Do you believe you're healing, or do you *know* when healing is making wholeness out of what was broken apart?

Your acceptance of the Atonement can only take place of you and by you. It is your destiny. Do you choose a life of false ideas, unsettledness, and anxiety, or a life of truthful healing? It's up to you. Once you do accept your truthful self, it is set forever as the thought extending from God. You are the Idea of Creation. Without the wholeness of you the Kingdom is bereft, and Creation is lacking. This is why your true free will is so important. It's your extension from God.

This gives you the vision to see everything about who you are. You even know when you are denying yourself. When you are doubtful you know, rather than believe. You know when you're not being yourself, and you know when you're living a fantasy or untruth. With this truth now being brought forward in you, the charade can be over. Let's face it. We do have a mission here. We're not passing through this dream of false ideas only to participate in the madness we tell ourselves is real.

Your Knowledge of Atonement

Let's not forget the goal we've accepted. It is more than just our own happiness alone we come to gain. What we accept as what we are proclaims what everyone must be along with us while we're in this dreamland. How so? Because the world we see around us is our projected images, made by our perceptions of what we think this world is all about. Given this condition, let's not fail our sisters and brothers, or we will certainly fail ourselves. This is how we may overcome the world, just as Jesus has modeled for us.

By your involvement in the Atonement you will be demonstrating the Oneness of God's Son. Your interwoven and integral part completes the Sonship and strengthens in unity. This is all that Jesus meant when He said, "Forgive them for they know not what they do." Humanity has been unaware of the wholeness that the Son of God truly is: that One Thought of God, which is your divinity. Your awareness of this without feeling obligated to *name* it is your acceptance of the Atonement.

This does not mean that you should run out all eager and in a hurry to tell all your friends and family that we all "make the Son of God whole and complete." Most likely you'll be seen as a pest—or worse—and not be taken seriously.

What you *can* do is simply be yourself, without a single false idea, and others will come to see the truth in you. They will want to be a part of it. They will want the same true confidence you have. Their minds will pick up on your mind, where Divine Truth abides and which will extend Itself. Your own *knowing* of this in the "name" of Creation is enough for you to share in the minds of others without even saying a word. This is so because you have the knowledge of wholeness everywhere.

I'd like to pass along a simple exercise that has helped me in my own acceptance of the Atonement. Try to make this become automatic in your daily routine, and it will, by using the following words in the form of a prayer or a brief meditation.

There have been times when I catch myself in awe, say, looking through the concertina wire fence around the prison yard and noticing a glorious sky, a rainbow, a sunrise or sunset, a blooming tree, or the simple landscape of farmland in the distance. I automatically repeat this statement:

This awe I feel inside is my knowledge of
accepting Atonement for myself. I remain as God created me.

Try this for yourself. Let it become automatic, so you use these words in your mind regularly. Create a style for doing so that feels right for you. You will know when the awe strikes you. You'll find it strikes you more and more often, at simpler and more unexpected times—not necessarily when you are gazing at the beauty of nature, but when you just take a step back and breathe in the hum of the world.

Now you're moving on and away from the caution zone, as you are at-one with the Atonement process. As you continue through this book, keep in mind that we are all involved in the Atonement, and the Holy Spirit is our Communicator. He will use you when the timing is just right in helping others accept Atonement for themselves. This may very well happen at times when you are totally unaware He is communicating through you to others.

Everyone's state of readiness and willingness is different, and His task within and through each of us is to know when the time is right. He certainly never fails. Let the Holy Spirit know when you are ready and willing, so that He may be the Judge on how to proceed. He knows what's best for you.

For example, as I was finishing this chapter, the feeling of being a victim to this prison system was ringing through me. Thoughts of being helpless as a convicted felon, which would limit my ability to one day help others in a style I can sometimes foresee, infiltrated inside me. I took a break from my writing tablet, stepped into the dayroom, and looked up at the television.

An interview with the famous movie actress Reese Witherspoon was airing on a Saturday morning talk show, in which she was speaking of her desire to help the world in the area of domestic violence. She stated that she would never have guessed that because of her career in Hollywood, doors would open for her to help make a difference in the world. Ms. Witherspoon's words sent a feeling through me that for the time being I was right where I needed to be. A calmness came over me, and I was okay.

Then I picked up my copy of *A Course in Miracles* and opened it directly, without effort, to page 565 in the text, and not so surprisingly read the following words:

The wish to be unfairly treated is a compromise attempt
that would combine attack and innocence.
Who can combine the wholly incompatible,
and make a unity of what can never join?

Chapter 16
Our Shared Certainty

Let's think for a moment of the way much of the world's population lives, how feeling alone, afraid, and threatened is sadly a fact we accept as life. It's been this way for millennia, and finding a way out of this trap in today's world seems to be getting tougher all the time.

It seems as though we are in a constant search to find even a few minutes of peace each day. We're afraid to risk ridicule if we stop and simply accept, and offer, peace from within, where it can only be found. We're in a mad rush to go out and about, and in the same mad rush to return home and shut the door behind us, hoping to settle into a quiet space that we believe will offer peace.

Our goal here and ahead is to shut the door permanently on being afraid in this world, to instead learn that giving opens an inner door to inner peace that quietly waits for us. Not only are we afraid to give, but we're also threatened by guilt that prevents our ability to receive, especially when it's someone we don't know doing the giving. This suspicious giving raises questions in our thought process. "I wonder what her ulterior motive might be?" Or, "If I accept this from her now, what am I getting myself into later?" And, "What's really behind this person's 'nice guy' act?"

These doubting-type thoughts and more are understandable suspicions to feel in the "dog-eat-dog" world we have made, and often we are bitten, leading to further defense. But you're not alone in feeling this way, and you don't need to feel afraid and threatened, because there is peace within you. It's there for you each moment of every day, regardless of the conflict and unsettledness you see all around you. It begins by being certain, because certainty is what you are, and when you are certain of yourself, forgiveness opens the door to the realm where peace exists. How so? Because when you forgive, you overlook the ego by looking beyond it. All that is left to tell is peaceful.

Our Reciprocal Nature

Almost everyone has learned to act reciprocally in a relationship where giving and receiving is involved. The thinking seems to be that returning a favor is the appropriate thing to do, so that we may display our gratitude and continue the flow of giving and receiving. On the surface level of who we are, this seems to be the right-minded approach in caring for our friends, family members, neighbors, coworkers, and others who help us out.

The power in the Creation of God, which is all about giving and receiving, is without limit and is not intended to be reciprocal. It can't be. We do, however, communicate fully with God, as He surely does with us. God inspires us through our Guide and Communicator, the Holy Spirit, so that we can create like Him. Our power is like His, but it does differ.

A Course in Miracles teaches us that "To think like God is to share His Certainty of what you are, and to create like Him is to share the perfect Love He shares with you."

As you become certain of yourself, you'll notice the Holy Spirit leading you to joy in a way only you could know. Your own true free will makes you complete because it brings you joy, and in this joy you are whole. Your wholeness is the Kingdom of Heaven, and each individual has a different free will, which gives them joy. It is still the same joy we all share, and this is Heaven.

As we've already said, there is a constant, continuous, uninterrupted flow of love between you and your Creator, much like electricity. This is the same love within the whole Sonship, and is why the Son of God is whole. God's Son is the whole power of the entire Creation. There is nothing magical or mythical about it. The Power and God are the same.

Love is given and received between ourselves and God, in one continuous thought. The giving and receiving is in the Power of God. In other words, as we give and receive love among one another, the sharing is the act of God. We are of this realm in the giving and receiving aspect involving each other. Reciprocation has nothing to do with it. But in the actual giving and receiving, it is not only "your" love or "my" love. It's the oneness I share with you as I receive your gift.

Cocreating

Sharing this realm of giving and receiving can be understood more clearly by the following life-changing circumstance that has raised in me a loving excitement. At this time, as I am writing this book—the rough draft, in its early stages with much yet to do before greeting a publisher—my oldest daughter, Erin, is in her early stages of pregnancy with her first child. This is a gift to me.

Erin is a beautiful thirty-two-year-old woman who sports a new, wonderful, and different glow about herself. Just like her own elation, even though I am behind bars in prison, I, too, have a different glow about myself, as a soon-to-be first-time grandfather.

I am eager to set my eyes on this marvelous addition to my family. I'm waiting to be able to hold my grandchild in my arms, even though, for now, it will have to be arranged in the prison visiting room. The glow we each behold is the same love I spoke of in the previous paragraphs, which appears in different respects. For certain it is the same glorious joy Erin and I share.

I, of course, cannot hold the same sensations as my daughter. She is feeling her baby move, and all of the nourishment she gives the baby through her body, along with all the other wonders and changes in her body she senses as the baby grows to full term.

On the other hand, Erin cannot possibly feel the sensation that comes over me as I see my once-little, cute, sweet girl in pigtails and missing front teeth now becoming a mother. This awe intensifies as I remember her first steps at nine months old, her first solo bike ride at age seven, her first school dance, her teenage years as a cheerleader for the high school teams, and so on. This joy and elation that consumes me is a positive force helping me through my dark times here in prison. Another gift.

But my point, in the sense I've just described, is that if we in our wholeness created God, and He also created us, the Kingdom could never increase through extension of its own creative thought. If this were so, creation would be limited, and no one would be a cocreator with God. But isn't this what our separated wrong-mindedness tries to do—that is, wishes to create God in our likeness through our own ego interpretations? In reality, of course, these false ideas of God get us nowhere, and they are why history continues to repeat itself.

Let's back up a moment to my daughter and all the love involved here. She and her new child are partly of me, but I will never be partly of them. My grandchild may one day have children and grandchildren, also partly of me, just as I am of my own parents, grandparents, and so on. In this sense, Erin and her offspring are cocreators with me, just as humanity as a whole is cocreator with God. We seem to hide from God's creative thought as *it* proceeds from Him to us. We seem to turn away from what we truly feel within and look for salvation outside of ourselves.

His thought is Creation and is the only way creative power can extend deeply inward and not outside of us. It continues through each of us, because we are *the extension* of that which is extended as total One-mindedness. God's accomplishments are not ours, but ours are like His, as we create "in His Likeness."

Chapter 17
Claiming the Power of Extension

Divinity cannot be defined in sizes, such as a maximum or minimum, increasing or decreasing, large or small. These are merely words assigned by humankind for our use, but as we discussed earlier, let's focus our attention on the meaning behind words. For example, when I say that God created the Sonship and we "increase" it by forgiveness, this is to define the efficiency or intensity of its wholeness as we perceive our progression to full Atonement, or total reawakening as a whole. Remember, each of us is in a different state of readiness and willingness to awaken from the dream of separate realities.

We increase wholeness by being both ready and willing to overlook the ego by looking beyond the obscurity, to where the Light that radiates in all of us can be seen. When Forgiving Light is obscured we are held back, and limited in our ability to recognize the power of the whole Sonship everywhere, which is our individual power. Once we can effortlessly look beyond wrong-minded actions, only then do we automatically experience right-minded thoughts and perceptions, and in due time effortless shifts to knowledge.

One-mindedness is total knowledge, where beliefs are not necessary because they don't exist. As we open ourselves from within, without fear, to the truth and knowledge we are all created from, the Kingdom increases. The more Heaven increases in its wholeness, the closer you will be to your own reawakening. The less you dream of separateness, the more whole you become. The real world in its wholeness is always at its maximum, and it comes to you as you gradually awaken.

Realizing the Confusion as Unreal

What does all of this really mean to you individually, and in the life you lead, when all most of us want is to get the most out of it? It means you don't have to live each day in fear, or feeling threatened by the inevitable end to it all. It means you can relax in the responsibilities you have accepted, and let life come to you. The extension of wholeness will find its way to you, and there's no need for the anxiety, stress, and hurried type of momentum you think you must live by.

Each of us has the ability to claim the power of extension when we become alert to the signs of communication by the Holy Spirit, which is God's Thought extending to you.

If you have not already, you will have the same or similar ego questions that have risen in all of us at one time or another. For example, "Why does God send out signals or signs to us when He could simply speak to us plainly in our own given language?" Or, "If He created me in His image, why doesn't he simply appear before me, where I can see Him, so we can have a face-to-face conversation? After all, He is capable of anything."

These are good, honest questions, but they arise from the confusion of the ego mind. These are thoughts concerning the body; they are questions of the body being asked by the body.

Remember, when humanity as a whole decided to separate from Oneness, it was a separation of mind and not of body. Our dream state in this instant, the nanosecond of projected bodily images that make the world we see, is of our own image-making—not God's. Sure, God did create us in His Likeness of Mind, but the body is our own self-made fantasy fashioned to hide our guilt from separating. Besides, it's all a dream.

Try to begin understanding that God does not extend Himself as a projected image. We've made our own image of God. While projections are necessary as the essence of any dream, *He* is not dreaming. The fantasy of a body as who you are does not carry with it a mind. Minds do not have actual physical features, such as a mouth or vocal cords to speak through. We are the extension of God's Mind, not of a body. This is why God uses his Holy Spirit, which is already in our minds, to communicate this realm of One-mindedness. He uses time, which we made, to do so.

This extension of God does not have any involvement with time, because time is a part of the dream. Our own capabilities of extending take place among all of us, regardless of the dream. When we do awaken wholly, time will have meant nothing. It's the nanosecond that is the duration of ego-life.

Since all minds are one, or altars if you will, within the One-Minded realm, then our power to extend (communicate) within this Oneness is seen as miracles in the dream. Are you with me here? If so, you are now experiencing the Oneness of Mind in the Real World, or true reality. However, the ego is quick to interrupt. If you're not with me here, even briefly, that's okay, because if you have a willingness, within time *Oneness* will come to you.

If you're having trouble with this, your willingness is proven by the fact of your effort. Therefore, throw out the effort by seeing your willingness as God's extension.

A Willing Participant

God's extension is eternity. But some equate eternity and its infinite realm to the solar system of planets, stars, and the clusters of galaxies hanging in space like bunches of grapes on the vine. Scientists have said that these clusters of separate galaxies hold individual galaxies totaling hundreds of thousands, and are vast light-years away from one another.

This is nothing more than a projected image as well, however, while we dream. If we're not there to witness it, does it truly exist? Anything of the physical is a projected image, and is thus of the separated mind. And why does the separated mind project images and wish to see them as real? Very good, if you've answered, "To hide the guilt" of our chosen separate identities from that of our Source.

Only that of God is eternally real. Anything else may seem real, but only inside of time. This tells us, therefore, that time is unreal.

By accepting the power to extend, and not your body, as being "what you are," you will have gained the knowledge to remember, and see through the fog of the dream to the Light of your real Self. This is your vision, your knowledge that strengthens the interlocking chain of Atonement. You begin seeing yourself as a willing participant, and others who are also willing participants will find you. This puts you in control of your true free will.

What are the creations you are capable of, that belong within you? It's certainly all the love you extend by living a life of purpose. This purpose that has come to you from your true free will is what creates miracles. To create is to love, and love extends because it cannot be contained.

The fact that my physical body is in prison (contained) does not in any way stop or limit my love extending to my daughter while she nourishes her pregnancy. Being that we have no limits, our extensions never stop. They are eternal and infinite. The true Self, which is beyond the body, is only love, and can only be of God, where time and space don't exist. Time means nothing in the extension of love, because it extends regardless of space and time, and love is not an image our egos can project. Ask a child to draw a picture of love and see what you get.

God Doesn't Make Bargains

The ego, which cannot recognize love, always demands reciprocal rights, because it is competitive; its goal is always to gain something. There is no love in this type of reciprocation. Bargains are always ready to be made, but the ego doesn't understand that to gain you must give in a realm where bargains have no meaning at all.

Any bargain is limited giving. This is not God's Will, and He has never made a bargain, nor will He ever. But haven't we been taught to make bargains with God in our prayers? Don't we see bargaining plans for Heaven going on everywhere? This is because the ego believes it can use sacrifice as a bargaining tool to gain Heaven.

Heaven is love and joy, and this can't be negotiated.

What the ego will never accept is that once we have awakened from this ever-so-brief lapse into separated thought, the daze or dream of life, we'll then realize we've been Home in the Kingdom all along. There's no need for bargains.

Is this an arrogant way of thinking? Only as interpreted by the ego, which turns its face from truth, or tries to debate it. The ego wishes to argue that the body is everything. But when we overlook its dreaming state, we can look beyond its unreality to our true reality. This is the forgiveness that erases guilt bit by bit until guilt is no more. Consider this: Has anything you ever dreamed of while sleeping in bed at night, awakened with you in the morning to then be seen as real? Hardly. But didn't you say, "Wow, thank God it was only a dream!"

Try to see your true free will as His gift to you while you dream of time and space. This free will of yours is an extension of His Will that has no limits, and its purpose is the functions you perform in the dream that slowly and gently help you and others to reawaken to where time is nonexistent. The time here is just a blink or flicker of the eyelids as you dream while your Father looks in on you.

If there were limits to your free will, this would be placing boundaries around God. This must tell you of your limitless nature in order that you become what you are capable of. Our creations, which are not subject to space and time, add to Heaven just as His Creation adds to you and me.

Jesus has taught us this, and what I've just explained is the Holy Spirit's reinterpretation of "I gave only to the kingdom because I know that Love is what I am."

What we have knowledge of determines our gifts and our creations. If God created each of us by extending Himself, which is who we are, then we can only extend ourselves as He continues to do so. This extension, we said, increases forever, since joy and eternity are inseparable. God extends through us and beyond all time, which for now we find difficult to grasp, but only because of our separated concept of time and space, and our projections of a material world.

The exciting part in all of this, however, is that as we continue to cocreate, or extend our love with God, the Holy Spirit carries our extensions around the world beyond all comprehension. Remember, He oversees the entire fragmented dream, in addition to helping you see beyond those dark circles under your eyes when you look in the mirror on a chaotic morning. So even with your limited comprehension you can relax, because your Guide will translate all of your extensions into peace and joy, a language everyone can understand, and which is the formula for forgiveness.

Next we'll move forward to learn to seed forgiveness by overlooking the ego. By doing so, we can deeply root forgiveness by looking beyond the ego's illusions and trickery, which promote error and the many misunderstandings of the world.

When this includes our personal and family lives, overlooking the ego by looking beyond it is necessary, making it possible and easy to forgive. This forgiveness, and its definition, is how we develop the peaceful comprehension we need, and it gives us the same certainty we share with God. It makes things happen in our lives—such as *miracles*.

PART III
LIVING WITH CERTAINTY

Chapter 18
The Certainty of Your Extension

If we can look at the return journey to reawakening as the healing process of the split-mind, as well as the healing of the guilt for the separation that plagues us, life can seem much easier for us. When something has split away and then has returned to its original wholeness, it has been healed.

Anything that has been truly transformed has healed because it was meant to be whole and not separate. Consider when you have injured yourself, such as a cut to the skin that has scabbed over and then cleared itself without scarring. The skin has become whole again and no longer separated, where it is exposed to germs. In this sense we can say the ego is the bacteria that keeps the mind from healing.

While this process is taking place, are we really thinking about every aspect of the healing process? No, we're not. But we can say that when we do heal in any form, it is the Thought of God slowly returning us to the original state of mind we can call Home.

Healing as a Correction

When you perceive yourself as sick, you are perceiving yourself as not being whole, thus being in need of something. If I also perceive you as lacking wholeness, meaning that I judge you poorly, then I must be without wholeness as well. The wholeness I speak of here is your totality, or Heaven, where sickness and separateness cannot abide.

Why? Because any separated thoughts are uncertain and are therefore not real. They are of time and space, which you project from your dream state of mind. Heaven is both real and is certain, and is the Truth of all that exists. Uncertainty is not truthful, which means it can't be eternal.

In this sense, then, to heal must be the correction of a wrong-minded perceived notion within yourself, and in me, by the communication of the Holy Spirit as the *link* between our minds. This linkage is a creation that brings us closer to that One-mindedness that is the eternal and infinite realm of wholeness. Our sharing the Holy Spirit as the linkage places us both in Heaven. Sharing of spirit reflects all of creation, because the links become no longer links at all and are unified as the whole One-Mind by the extension of each other and to each other. In this process we all extend and are receiving at the same time.

What we project only seems to be real and will one day be gone when time has ended. But what we extend is not governed by time and is real while time lasts and beyond. For instance, can I extend love to my daughter while she dreams in her sleep? Something that extends already exists in that very instant in which it is being extended, regardless of a dream state of mind. This is a law of the mind that has never changed and never will.

Assumptions as Knowledge?

Let's consider our state outside of Heaven, which is where these projections are made. We see these manmade laws prevailing inside our idea of Heaven, based on what the "separate wholes" of the ego mind project as their beliefs. These disparate beliefs are fragmented and argumentative, unable to portray an accurate picture of this realm of paradise.

Our traditional beliefs tell us that only outside of Heaven is learning essential, so that we may one day get there. We believe we must try to learn or find what it is we truly are, rather than merely being it. Based on the past and present projections of others, perpetrated as lessons about ourselves, we form a belief system based on presumptions instead of true knowledge. Can you see the world as presumptuous much of the time, where it thinks it is knowledgeable?

Try now to look inside of Heaven, where there is no such thing as teaching or learning, and certainly not a single presumption. There are no beliefs inside of Heaven, where certainty is all that exists. In the certainty of true wholeness, God and His entire Sonship knows that you extend what you are. This form of law, which constitutes oneness, does not need to be adapted to fit circumstances, because oneness is only certain and has no circumstances to contend with. This is real natural law.

There is nothing that can oppose total oneness, when oneness is the natural law of the Kingdom of Heaven. God not only created it but He is also created by it. To extend is to create, and when we create we communicate by being who we truly are, which involves using the wholeness of which we are.

Translating Meaning

Laws cannot be helpful unless they are communicated and therefore understood. Laws must be translated for those who speak different languages. A good translator must alter the form of what he translates, while being careful not to change the meaning. The whole purpose is to change the form so that the original meaning is retained.

You are with me here in certainty if you can see that the Holy Spirit is our translator of the laws of God, for those who don't understand them. Due to the conflict in our minds we cannot do this for ourselves while being faithful to one meaning. We would end up changing the meaning to preserve the form based on what we were taught to believe.

Keep in mind that the Holy Spirit's purpose in translating is exactly the opposite to that of this world. He translates only to preserve the original meaning in all respects and in all projections of understanding, in any language—domestic, foreign, or even slang. He opposes the idea that differences in form are meaningful, emphasizing always that these differences don't matter.

God's law of creation doesn't involve teaching us the truth. Creation *is* truth and is what we are. You are what you are, and learning this is not necessary to know this fact. However, when humanity separated its thought from God and developed its own thought system, there was no choice but to become a learner as a necessity for survival. This "necessity" survives today. Could this be why we are considered to be "creatures of habit?" Why is it we never question the connection between learning something new and memory? How can we learn without a memory?

This is why the Holy Spirit teaches us His lessons in remembering and in forgetting. But the forgetting part of His lessons is only to make the remembering consistent.

Why do you suppose you can't remember God, let's say, as in before you were born? The answer is because you're not able to forget the ego in order that you truly can remember who you are.

We can't possibly understand the Holy Spirit's translations while we're involved in the conflict of two different ways of interpreting them. Our ego-based thought system by which we live surely conflicts with real, unseparated thought, which is the thought system of certainty the Holy Spirit uses. Therefore, we must surrender one in order to understand the other. This is truly the only way we can learn to be consistent in truth, so that we can once and for all be certain about ourselves.

If you are operating from the thought system that confuses you and keeps you indecisive, what then can the perfect consistency of Heaven mean for you? If we maintain the ego as our direction, we experience confusion in how we interpret certain things, because we try to dissect them rather than appreciate them. Whatever we appreciate extends its value.

Whenever you operate from certainty there is no confusion, because there's only *one* certain meaning. One thing for certain is that your body cannot extend, but it can project an image of itself. A thought, however, if it is real—which means external and not of time—infinitely extends and rests on its idea. It's the Idea of Creation, which is whole and never separated—that is, it is of your real life.

Chapter 19
Conflict Seeks Allies

On a gloomy morning a confused student went to the schoolmaster and asked a question that had been weighing heavily on his mind: "What is the method of liberation?"

The wise old master, with a whimsical and experienced smile, replied, "Who binds you, my son?"

The student proudly answered, "No one binds me."

The master squarely met the young man's eyes and said, "Why, then, should you seek liberation?"

By being conflict-free, you can maintain maximum efforts and will receive maximum results. In this peak performance, what is considered to be maximal effort is really effortless.

Think of the times when you were at peak levels of performance. Wasn't it effortless? There was no exertion or strenuous or anxious thoughts going on. The experience seemed to flow, and whatever resources were needed to accomplish your faithful mission just seemed to show up.

Your Peak Level Now

You are at a peak level whenever you surrender all conflict within yourself, and the Holy Spirit takes over in your right-mind, giving you a lesson. In all situations there are lessons being learned, which are important in your function while here on Earth, whether you realize it or not. Even that one spectacular round of golf, where your shot making was flawless and seemed to prevail in a performance much greater than your usual play, did indeed have something to teach you.

Or how about the words that seemed to unexpectedly flow from you when a friend or family member needed them the most? Or that business decision that was firmly and confidently made that boosted the morale of your employees, yourself, your family, and bumped up your company's bottom line? These situations are being handled for you by the Holy Spirit for reasons in you, and in others, that may not be necessary for you to understand in their entire scope. You are being told what to do, and all you need to do is be alert to its possibilities. You'll learn when it's the right time to take some type of action.

His message is to be conflict-free all the time, which will leave room for maximum performance. For example, in that great round of golf there cannot be a situation where your body is in conflict with your mind as to how to execute the golf shot. It is the same when you encourage a friend, son, or daughter to make a decision that is right for them. You cannot be in conflict with the words you choose or in the feelings you have regarding the matter.

The peak performances you experience in these instants, without conflict, are glimpses of Heaven. What really are these "instants" I speak of? They are the timeless series of nanoseconds in which you meet the Real World. You've been there. We all have.

Exactly how this is achieved doesn't matter, because if it did and we chose to dissect it like an engineering project, conflict would enter into its formula—for example, striving to improve on it. Striving is conflict. The no-time zone of "now," called Heaven, is always maximal, and getting there is your consistent journey through periods of physical time that are as free as possible of conflict. Being in the "now," with no hint of past or future, is always at peak level, and is the ideal state of mind. Nothing can outperform what you do in the no-time zone of *now*.

Never Absent and Always within Us

When our elder brother, Jesus, said, "I am with you always," He meant it literally. He was aware of the Christ-Mind in Himself and in everyone. At the time, two thousand years ago (an instant ago), Jesus was aware of the role of the Sonship and recognized that His function and purpose was to lead the way.

He spoke of this through His parables in the best way He could, to spark the interest of those during that time. The man, Jesus, an image in the dream projected from guilt, was able to manifest the Holy Spirit of God by His awareness of it. His leadership and His image and behavior, as a model for Truth, is what manifests the Holy Spirit in each of us today. Some of us are aware of this, and others are not. But more are learning each day of this capability.

This is why I urge you not to discount, as an example of this, that super round of golf where effortless joy is brought forward in your mind. Or that kind set of words that truly helped a friend through a tough day. Or the responsibility my good friend Ron took upon himself to help see me through the dark times prison offers. These are experiences of wholeness of mind serving a purpose, whether in a game like golf or the more serious matters. You must look at the psychology in this, rather than the body's participation. We can call the mind behind this psychology Christ.

Christ is not a body, never absent, and is within us always, because it is who we are. Anything else is of the ego mind, a false idea of who we are that projects a body to hide from guilt. All that can exist is either of truth or falsehood, real or unreal, the Christ-Mind or ego-mind, and nothing is in between, or a middle ground. Because the Christ-Mind is always who we are in reality, Jesus wanted us to know that we are "the Way, the Truth, and the Life."

We did not make this power any more than Jesus did. It was created to be shared, and does not, nor ever has or ever will, belong to any particular individual alone. Through the Christ-Mind is how we communicate, and it is extended by the Holy Spirit, available for our tapping into at any given time. It is the shared inspiration, the One Thought of the One Mind, which is Creation.

The meaning behind the word "Christ" waits in Heaven, or within us, where God placed it, and once you have experienced it, you will know that it does not hang around waiting in time for some special event in the future to free us. Christ belongs where He is, and that place is within you. But once again, I must remind you that I am not speaking of "within" your body.

You Already Possess What You Need

We must begin to become aware that the ego tries to teach us that we are not what we really are. The ego tells us we are arrogant to see ourselves as of the Christ-Mind. In fact, the ego strives to focus on Christ as a human body, and it sees the body as reality.

For example, don't we all question the reality of a spirit? The ego has its lessons that we cannot whole-mindedly share with others, because it's impossible to totally agree and share with someone thoughts that are so fragmented and split apart and separate. If it's not whole it's not about who you truly are. Besides, the ego doesn't believe in unity or sharing unless it has potential gain hooked to it. This is why the ego is always in conflict of something and can never be whole.

Consider a conversation consisting of small talk, when you'd like to share an accomplishment with someone. Have you ever tried to share something about yourself—say, the huge bass you caught on a fishing trip, or your daughter's pregnancy—only to find the other person turning the conversation to his own fishing trip, and with a bigger fish, or her own daughter's fancier wedding? Not only does the listener wish to top your story, but he or she causes you to judge him or her. This is because separate egos have nothing that can be shared, except judgments of each other and of other individuals.

The ego's premise in you is consistently being corrected and reversed by the Holy Spirit, and His cultivating of your ground consists of the undoing of errors, where right-minded "seeds are being sown." The ego feels the threat of peace toward its domain, where oneness is blending its way into your whole mind. This is what the ego fights against.

This is why the ego tries to make part of you its friend and seeks your help as an ally in the conflict. The real you does, indeed, recognize an individual for his conflict-free side. You are already in possession of everything you need, and with this abundance you have no need to "outperform" anyone. But on the other hand, if you perceive an individual as not equal to you, it is only because you see his ego through the eyes of your own ego. You're not seeing him through real vision, or the Christ-Mind, and there is an absence of brother-to-brother sharing.

Somewhere along the way you began operating from wrong-mindedness. When this is the case, which it will often be, simply take note of this in your mind, and have faith that right-mindedness will soon be ushered in by the Holy Spirit. This is merely a part of the healing process, so make sure you understand it as such. Then you can tell yourself, quietly, calmly, and in peace, to "let bygones be bygones." Next, you must move on by chalking it up as a lesson given you by your Guide on the path to Atonement. And there is another step to understand.

All of our conflicts stem from our need to be vigilant against our own interests. If your interests are of your own free will, however, then there is no need to feel that conflicting interests are ever possible. If you're not living your life around your free will, you are in fear of many things. This is because you fear your own death.

What does fearing death have to do with your conflicts? It's simply the ego in you, advising and rushing you to "get all you can because you can't take it with you." You're afraid you won't *get* enough before the obituary runs in the newspaper.

It's easy to perceive ourselves as lacking when death is our number-one fear. We can certainly become uncertain in this state. It shows in everything we do. But when you're certain about the "now," there are no uncertainties over having "bigger fish to fry."

Chapter 20
The Gathering Place

Consider the age-old question of loyalty. "If you can't count on your brother, who can you count on?" We'd surely like to think we can count on the trustworthiness of a brother or sister. But I'm not primarily meaning your siblings' help with material forms of assistance. We've all seen failure, here on Earth, because too much emphasis is placed on the body.

I am, however, writing about the knowledge we all have of our own existing right-mindedness. It's the knowledge you have that there is a good, positive side of yourself and in everyone you encounter. This knowledge, which you share with everyone on some level, rests inside of Truth. It's the positive force of Truth that many choose to tap into, though others do not. Many operate their lives from the wrong-mindedness of a fabricated truth they erroneously believe enables them to gain success in material form.

We can "count on" or trust other individuals as having the same right-minded side that's in ourselves, which represents the Light of who they are, whether he or she realizes it or not. Everyone senses a belonging or a connection to that same Truth, our Source, which we share as one magnificent Light.

By showing your own stable footing as rooted in truthful types of thoughts, others will pick up on this extension of you and sense the fact that they have the same ability. They will see their own reality in your truthful demeanor. It's in this wholeness that miracles are created, which can only occur behind the seemingly brave front of the ego many of us display, though it's nothing more than a disguise we think hides our faces.

The wholeness is the depth of yourself. It's the truthful side in you of the split-mind that sincerely asks, "How are you doing this morning?" or sincerely congratulates a friend for a great round of golf without having an ulterior motive; for example, "buttering up" a contact to gain a business deal. This Truth about you, and the same in another, is a glimpse of your brotherhood. However briefly it may show its colors, it is a tie to the Little

Garden Society.

This part of the mind in all of us we all share in Truth. This is where the Society gathers; or we can call it the mindful gathering place, free of ego infestation. No wishful thinking here. Trust in yourself is essential in establishing your own abilities to extend yourself, rather than projecting images only to sustain the beliefs you made for interacting in a frightening world.

Using real vision to understand your own wholeness will transcend your doubts, leaving you free from fear, or at least realizing why you are fearful over any given situation. It's the doubts our projected images give us of others that bring on attackful types of thought. But you have the power to relinquish thoughts of attack that you once erroneously believed were necessary for your own survival.

Shifting the Focus Gradually

What are we really doing whenever we attack someone, whether in thought, verbally, or physically? It's simple. We're telling ourselves that he or she is limited by our own perceived projections of the way this individual appears to us, or how we wish they would act or appear while in our presence. Is there any loyalty of brotherhood in this?

We think that these wishful perceived notions of others will ensure our security. But what's really happening is that our wrong-mindedness is afraid to make the shift over to Truth, and that we are also afraid to look beyond the errors of others, as well as ourselves. This becomes a block to our own awareness of the real Self that stands right-mindedly behind our errors, which is a step below total One-mindedness.

The Little Garden Society's gathering place is inside this One-mindedness, or Christ-Mind, and it gently whispers down to the right-mind, keeping us—in a positive manner—informed and alerted to the untruths of the world and where they sit. Here is where the Holy Spirit communicates in the right-mind so that we may help others shift over to unity as a way of thinking and perceiving situations.

This is how the Society helps one another and the rest of the world to understand that overlooking ego-based behavior will give the world freedom to look beyond the illusory foundation humanity has built, which is wrong-minded wishful thinking. This is why, for the most part, the world is presumptuous when it thinks it is being knowledgeable.

Jesus spoke of this when He told us about the two men who built their houses. One built his house on sand, while the other dug deep (within) until he hit solid rock (Truth). Remember, Jesus taught through parables. This story in particular, and many others of His friendly conversations, was His way of bringing forward the right-minded perception in folks. Jesus knew it was a way his listeners could see for themselves what they were capable of.

Any perception we have from the right-mind stems from a focus that tells us what we think we *want* to see. This is positive. If we can shift this focus gradually to a knowledge of what we want, which is what Jesus was helping folks to do through His parables, then what we see changes accordingly. The vision will shift to make wholeness-of-mind the focus.

The Little Garden Society gathers only in wholeness, everywhere, with those who are recognizing that right-mindedness is where the shift to knowledge occurs. But we must help the world realize this. It's simple; a positive willingness brings out the knowledge in you, because you must operate in Truth to help others.

How do we know and teach others to simply follow the Truth within them? By taking action in example setting and not by running around suggesting to everyone you see to "give love," or by placing ads in the newspaper or on television that insist we must "Praise the Lord." The Lord does not want us to praise Him, because He has no ego that needs attention. There are a number of pesty practices in our faces daily that only try to build an image of the ad owner as strong, when really they are afraid.

If we can see Jesus as our True model of a right-minded approach to living life, then we can easily step up to the knowledge of One-mindedness and become involved in real miracle-mindedness. The reawakening to One-mindedness is your resurrection, which is the mind dawning on what it truly is. Additionally, can you imagine Jesus if He were here today, running all kinds of advertisements selling salvation?

Of course that question is merely my attempt to help you think with humor about the Truth much of the world denies and for you to realize that you do indeed extend yourself without the need to say a word or sell yourself.

The key is to remove your focus from your brother's so-called sins. This will remove the obscurity that will give the glow of peace within and around you that others will recognize. Others will recognize this "halo effect," so to speak, from their own right-mindedness, the same part in you, and then it will be brought forward in their own mind. This is no different from the reasons why Jesus used parables and taught by example.

What the Right-Mind Does Not See

I hope your real vision is seeing that what we're after here is the real meaning behind the method of communication we choose to use. It's the meaning in this book—specifically how it pertains to you—that is the guiding force to help you see the real you.

When others sense your right-mindedness, they have found their own and will be part of what you're extending. To focus on mistakes or errors as sin is like focusing on weeds in the garden as the evil that deprives the garden of beauty. Rather, we can gently and quietly remove (undo) the weeds without any motive other than the growth and beauty of the garden. The weeds are seen as reversible errors for whatever reason that initiated them.

To focus on sin is to focus on illusions. Why? Because you are focusing on the dream instead of reality. There is no such thing as sin in the *real world*. But there are errors in our thought process that made the dream project itself in how you see sin. Even with the murderer, like the ones I am here with in prison, living side by side—my right-mind does not see these individuals as murderers, but my ego does see them as a body that took an innocent human body's life, and the projection of that image plays out accordingly. But did someone really lose a life? Did a murder actually happen? To the ego and the dream of bodily form, yes, it did. But is this real?

I do realize this is a hard pill to swallow, and understandably so, by the ego in you that is trying to be in control of your thinking over this idea of murder not being sinful. Does this mean we should condone any such attack? Not at all. But forgiveness lies in seeing the sinlessness of the murderer from behind the dream, by looking beyond it. You can start now to let all such sinless focuses make a path for your own sinlessless to be seen. What does this mean, and what can you do?

I'm saying here to let others see who you are behind the dream of sin, and without advertising it. You will set an example. It might seem like a slow process and an uphill battle, but this is what will reduce the number of murders inside the dream of time and space. Only the ego sees difficulty in this.

The sinlessness that you are is your right-minded way of living on the earth, and this way of living is already catching on around the world everywhere. The fearful, wrong-minded thoughts that spur on your wrong-minded perceptions make you see a garden of weeds.

If we stop being so anxious about the future, and regretful or blaming over the past, and put our right-mindedness into trusting the same in others, our extension of love will override projected, unreal thought. The dream will seem to fade. Once this happens we can begin to see a brother in time of need, and the whole Sonship expands to make room for him to join. Events start being arranged because of the need in this world for his or her true free will. Try to look and see what is behind the ego-based thoughts of others. You'll be surprised how easy it is to use real vision here.

Our Worrisome Concerns

A major hazard to the success we seek has been the involvement with the past and our future goals. Many of us also concern ourselves too much with depressing thoughts. We may sense for the time being that the weeds are clear, but sure to return. We continue to project doom. How can this worry about what has not yet occurred really happen? It can't.

It's all a dream, and ego infestation is not real. These worrisome concerns are merely defenses against present change and the fear of a new focus. That's all it is. Why the fear? Because how we may project the future with this change of focus is uncertain, and what is not certain frightens the ego. But on the other hand, the *certainty* of Truth severely scares the ego. The ego is always afraid, no matter how certain or uncertain things may be.

This is a trap, and your release from it is to accept the fact that you live an eternal life, and eternity is certain. That said, you can now forget the past, and all worry about the future. The certainty is that your body will one day end its time here only because it is due time for you to experience reality, the real world. You can do this by letting go of all worry and frustration, and begin extending what you are, which is love. You can easily do this by simply being yourself.

The sinless right-minded thoughts of your brothers/sisters are as real as your own, and each of us shares the same fertile and rich soil of the Garden. This is why you are rich in mind.

None of us need allow anger to block our way. If a brother's sins come into your view of him, you've narrowed your focus, restricting your own real vision, thus seeing your own mistakes, and then potentially magnifying them as sins. With regard to past or future, when these blocks arise, simply transcend them by acknowledging the following words or work them into your normal prayers or meditations:

>It's not this narrow focus I want to see.
>Rather, I trust my brothers/sisters who share the Garden.

Remember, what you truly want will be given to you by the Holy Spirit, because it's necessary to attaining your true free will. It's your salvation.

Chapter 21
Forgetting So You May Remember

The true essence, the core to individuals everywhere, regardless of race, wealth, religion, nationality, or any other type of status structure the world assigns, is of the One Mind, which brings wholeness to you and your brother/sister. Oneness heals.

Wholeness is the conflict-free essence of the Son of God, and inner peace is the simplest understanding of its perfection. This perfectness is the certainty of God, where His Laws are certain and simple to understand. With inspiration from the Holy Spirit in you, healing is a result of these laws. Since we are the Holy Spirit from our right-mind, the inspiration we have for our free will continually reminds us it's also God's Will. This is why you can relax and let go of the past, by honoring the present as the key to the future.

We're too quick to think of healing in physical terms, but that's okay. Just use the physical sense you have to relate healing to the split-mind. In other words, equate the cut finger to the healing process ongoing in the mind. Consider the Laws of God as the antibodies rushing in to aid in your forgetting of ego illusions. When we forget, it is a way of remembering better. To forget is to clear away ego-based fog that obscures real vision.

But we have been taught to understand forgetting as the opposite of remembering. Opposites do conflict. However, if we perceive the process of forgetting properly it can be used as a way out of conflict, just as must be our goal with perception. As right-mindedness strengthens, it is undoing the wrong-mindedness of the ego.

The ego has never learned anything and surely does not wish that we realize it can never learn anything real. Such a wish would defeat its purpose. While it is impossible for the ego to learn anything, it is able to perceive "truth" as it wishes. The ego makes its choices based on this wishful thinking, and then claims it to be a lesson learned. Its own interpretations are used as its lessons in life, often based on formal education.

Don't get me wrong here. We indeed must educate our children, which is part of our responsibility in bringing forward a more right-minded way of the world. But how often do we use this formal education as a launching pad into wrong-mindedness, where corruption breeds actions for personal and material gain? The future adults who are our babies today can one day use their formal education to shift the world and increase a more permanent right-minded approach to interacting. But we must individually utilize our wholeness to lead the way now, so they can lead later. Material gain will come about abundantly as a result.

Bringing Truth Forward

The Holy Spirit takes a place in our right-mind to teach us to use what the ego has made, so we can understand these illusions for the nothingness they are, illusions that have been leading us astray from our own true free will. These errors, often seen as sins, are ultimately necessary for our growth and real learning.

Consider what the world sees as truths today, which generations ago were seen as falsehoods—or, conversely, what is seen as false today but were once viewed as truths that countries went to war over. Was truth really being unveiled or discovered during the Inquisition or Colonial witch hunts? Did truth really prevail during the Crusades, fought over religion, property, and wealth? Was truth brought forward when millions of Jews and others were slaughtered by Hitler and the Nazi Party that backed him? Did we learn anything as a result?

Many individuals around the world today continue to lose their lives or are physically imprisoned for disagreeing with or expressing opinions that are counter to the leadership in power, even when the laws of their land may not even have been broken. In this country, as well as others, individuals are being locked up for attempting to crack the hard shell of ego-based political policies. They end up in prison on trumped-up charges for crimes they did not commit.

Examples and case stories are everywhere, but the specifics of these causes are not what this book is about, so I will move on. However, I must admit I feel an urging starting to churn inside me to one day write such a book, about the possibility of overcoming such underhandedness resulting from wrong-minded goals.

I hope you're with me here in seeing this type of learning as being meaningless and helpless, unless it can result in newly brought-forward abilities that look beyond the ego-based efforts that make the world we try so hard to keep up with.

The belief in whatever is considered to be true often is a charade that lives on in households, businesses, courts of law, governments on all levels—federal, state, and local— and on and on. But for every wannabe truth, what is real in this world wins every time. All you need to do is to make the willingness in your heart to help a better world shine through the fog. Your potential will come forward and it will extend. This is the Holy Spirit's goal for all efforts, which He will instill in you as effortless.

Giving Him Your Abilities

If different abilities are applied consistently enough to one goal, the abilities themselves become unified. All minds become channeled in one direction, contributing to one result. The emphasis falls on similarities, not differences.

In other words, the whole Sonship, which includes the true free will of others, will find you to help in the mission of Atonement, where your unique function is needed. This is the Law of God, a true Universal Law governing over its Divine task.

This is why we must hand over all of our abilities, along with our disabilities or confusion, to the Holy Spirit, who understands how to use them properly. He will use them for healing because He knows each of us as whole, which is the same as your knowledge of being a whole Son of God. It's the part of you that knows there is more to who you are than the dream of a separated Father and Son.

The Holy Spirit uses our abilities to teach us of wholeness as we all shift and direct our thinking more inwardly, which begins in the right-mind. By being aware of the need to be whole, in that alone we are remembering God. Our remembrance of Him has been obscured by the false ideas of the ego, which has offered us its own perception, and we've chosen to buy into it.

A cute story as a good example of this occurred with my good friend here in prison. Bob is eighty-two years old. His wife of a similar age passed away a few years ago, while Bob was new to prison. When he is released from prison, which is to be soon, Bob says the first thing he must do is purchase a double cemetery plot for himself and his already-buried wife. His plan is to have his wife's remains moved to the newly purchased gravesite. His wish is that when he passes on, the two of them will be side by side in Heaven.

You may be chuckling slightly over Bob's thought process. But isn't this similar to the beliefs much of the world holds regarding an eternity, with the body as the main focus? Of course there are loving, right-minded intentions in Bob's thinking. So what is the lesson? you may be asking.

The Holy Spirit will translate forgetting into a way of remembering. My right-mindedness sees Bob as sensing *oneness* of mind, and this is simply his way of expressing it. He's tapping into a knowledge that tells him he is already at-one with his wife, but for symbolic purposes, moving her body so they can be buried together allows him to see oneness in action, the only way he can express it to himself. Regardless, Bob is tapping into unity, or the knowledge of it. But don't rely on what I see in Bob's goals here; please examine what you see yourself.

Always Uniting and Healing

Let's look closer at the ego for what it really is, which is nothing but a bundle of errors, split and fragmented into uncountable and unrecognizable parts. The ego thinks it has a unified goal, just as the Holy Spirit does. But the ego can never reconcile with your Teacher's goal. At best, the ego can only fade away, and as it does it strives to buy more time. It does so by looking for ways to divide and separate even further.

But the Holy Spirit is constantly uniting and healing, which is the process of shifting to One-mindedness by way of the right-mind. Ultimately we will all achieve this, along with the rest of humanity, which is why I suggest we relax and enjoy the ride.

Consider a career choice where you may be on a wrong path. The prospect of having to make a change leaves you feeling incomplete, not to mention the stress and anxiety that go with it. Is it your perception, or is it your own knowledge of the incompleteness and misery that convinces you a change must be sought after? It may have started out when you perceived not-so-good feelings about your choice, until finally, after consistent efforts in your chosen career, you just came to *know* you much seek change, to something you will enjoy. To "en-joy" is to live in accordance not only with God's Will, but also your true desire, or free will.

A Course in Miracles sheds light on this type of situation: "To think you can oppose God's Will is a real delusion."

The ego will not concern itself with God's Will unless it's to threaten you with it. How many times in our lives, especially growing up, were we told to do things we really didn't want to do because it was said to be God's Will?

Remember, as discussed earlier in this book, the ego is not evil, but it is erroneous due to its lack of a knowledge it can never attain. Evil is only a projection of your fears. Why do we have fears? Due to the guilt we place on ourselves for believing that time and space are real, when deep down within and behind it all, we know the truth. The laws of the real universe are a gift, in that the more and more we operate from truth, the more we are able to see through the dream of projected images.

Using the Gifts

The One-mindedness of Creation is an incredible gift to each of us, in that we "have" and "are" everything we could ever need. When we don't use the gifts we were given, we are forgetting we have them. By not remembering these gifts, we don't know *what* we are and enter a state of confusion. Healing is the way of bringing on the perception that something is wrong, then shifting over to knowledge by thinking in accordance to God's Laws, causing ourselves to recognize that change is necessary.

For example, you may notice that a friend of yours is elated and complete in his or her career, and has a great income, a nice home, and luxury cars. You may witness this person doing all the fun things in life that you seem unable to afford to do. Your focus becomes more and more on the ball and chain that binds you in that prison of a job you have.

You're noticing jealousy in yourself toward your friend, and this alone disgusts you. But thanks to this person, this jealousy is an ingredient for the recipe that gets you thinking about your own needed change. The change you accept is your way of welcoming the whole to you. The whole has sought you out and is waving you in, just as you would welcome a single lone golfer who is a hole behind you on the golf course, asking that he join you.

You will receive *its* arrival once you have devoted yourself to seeking change. Now we can understand the Holy Spirit's reinterpretation of the Bible instruction: "Seek ye the Kingdom of Heaven." This is where the Laws of God operate truly in you, because *you* are the Kingdom of Heaven. Seek within yourself first; then you can function truly, because *you* are these Laws.

See yourself as Truth, which is what heals, and healing being the way of forgetting the sense of danger the ego has induced in us. While I was writing my first book based on the principles of *A Course in Miracles*, I was afraid and concerned about the judgment that would be made against me for its unconventional content. Only when a necessary shift in my perception of other peoples' outlook occurred could I foresee those who would welcome my message.

When perception is transformed to knowledge, the thought of danger fades away, leaving us with joy and confidence. The result is remembering what you are; you are here to remember God. By remembering you will awaken.

Chapter 22
Laying the Groundwork

A wise businessman into his later years, my good friend Bob Russell, who never retired, presented a few words to a graduating class of students ready to head out into the world. I'd like to share his words with you, since they are appropriate for discussion here.

"After a while you learn the subtle difference between holding a hand and chaining a soul. You learn that love doesn't mean leaning on someone, and company doesn't mean security. You begin to discover that kisses aren't contracts and presents are not promises. You begin to accept your defeats with your head up and your eyes open, with the grace of your spirit, not the grief of your ego. And you learn to build all your roads on today, because tomorrow's ground has yet to exist.

"After a while you learn that every sunshine burns if you get too much. So plant your garden to decorate your own free spirit, instead of waiting for someone to bring you flowers. And you learn that you really can endure, and that you really are strong just being who you are. After all these lessons you will see that you indeed have a purpose in this world. It's called being truly yourself."

Did you know that you can choose to leave this world entirely anytime you want? I'm not speaking of your physical death; I mean a change of mind in how you interpret the reality of this world.

Seeing Value in This World

If you believe this world has real value in helping you with your heroic mission, then it will remain of value to you. On the other hand, if you see no value in this world, and are filled with ridicule, and see doom and gloom everywhere, and see nothing in it that serves your purpose, then it will remain the dark dream or nightmare you continue to make for yourself. With myself, I have learned to turn the darkness of my incarceration into the light of a period of time to launch certain writing goals, as a pathway for completing myself.

How do you move on and make the necessary changes so that you may live a life of purpose and free will? Is this where you will find peace? Do you really want inner peace, happiness, security, and a certainty of purpose in life, leaving you with a sense of worth? Do you want to be understood and respected in the community? Do you want to be able to relax whenever you would like and never get upset?

Your answers to these questions are absolute. You do want these things, and this is how every person you've ever met would want to live. It's sad but true, however, that many individuals seem to do nothing in order to create this change and have it be possible.

Forgiveness offers you this wealth. You can wake up in the morning alert and with an aliveness that shows certainty of the day ahead of you. At bedtime you will anticipate your mission for the following day and have a restful night's sleep.

If I can learn this while living each day and night in a state prison, then you can certainly begin living the life that is truly what you want. Not what you wish for, but what you truly *want*. You will have joy to bring to your day and to others, merely by your purpose, which will make your presence light up. While you sleep you'll have no fearful dreams of insecurity and attack. You can accomplish this by overlooking the ego as you look beyond it, as well as beyond the dust the body will ultimately turn to. By looking beyond the illusions of this world, you'll see the reality that's within you. Then proceed from there.

Your Choice to See Beyond

A Course in Miracles brilliantly defines forgiveness in a way the ego-mind cannot keenly grasp, but that can penetrate the real you. "Forgiveness recognizes what you thought your brother did to you has not occurred. It does not pardon sins and make them real. It sees there was no sin. What is sin except a false idea about God's Son? Forgiveness sees its falsity and therefore lets it go. What then is free to take its place but the Will of God?"

Could this be teaching us that we can choose to see beyond the fog that covers our true essence, and that of our brothers and sisters, who may be seeing an unforgiving world? The world can surely be unforgiving if we choose to dwell on its darkness and see it as our doom. Forgiveness allows you individually to see yourself as the Son of God, who does not sin, because sin is only of the separated mind, which is not real. It's not real because it's not of God's Creation. Sin is only seen within the frame of time, a dream, the false idea of a world. Simply illusion.

Try to see that your errors in thought are projecting a dream separate from what my own errors project. Your errors are only errors, just as my own are, but they can be cleared away by the real unseparated, nondreaming Light that exists within both of us. It's the same Light that is our wholeness drawing the darkness of the ego to it, until it fades away before your real vision. True light, then, is all that is left to be seen.

This is what moves you when you let go of false ideas and allow the whole to consume all of you. With that said and accepted, forgive yourself and others for the errors made during the time spent in darkness. It's difficult for one to find his or her way in the dark. With your *forgiving light*, the whole not only comes to you, it becomes yours and is your wealth and abundance. We can say this is called "finding yourself."

To begin recognizing this motion, whatever it is you do truly want, simply accept it as already yours, and then proceed accordingly to carry out this function. God wants you to have it, because it is your true free will. Remember, though, that your body's desires are not your free will. The good news is that bodily pleasures just happen to come along with the ongoing accomplishments and in the process of attaining your mission in life.

The Confidence to Advance

Your life's purpose is meant to be enjoyed. You will know what is feasible and what is not. There are no other values you are deprived of that forgiveness will not bring to you. How is this? you might ask.

Once you can look beyond your own ego, what you desire you will receive if this is your sincere will, and your body benefits too, merely by going along with the process. Here, you can say, by overlooking the ego in yourself and seeing beyond its untrue ways of thinking, you are seeing and experiencing the peace of Heaven you so desperately have been seeking. You will then have the confidence to advance by allowing your faith to lead you to your own completeness. But your completeness cannot be attained until wholeness finds you and brings you in—and it will.

To say you want peace of mind and to live your free will is one thing, but to truly mean it *is* everything. If it is the intent of your true essence, then it will only take an instant for you to leave all indecisiveness behind. This is the timeless instant of reality, or Heaven, that the ego can never understand. It's that tickless, clock-free time period when you choose between truth and falsehood, real and unreal, Christ-Mind or ego-mind. It's in this instant that you set reality into motion as the whole Sonship greets you.

These decision-making instants are when you accept the decision to be real, and the Holy Spirit begins laying the groundwork, which will consist of contributions from the Whole Sonship. In fact, much of this may have already been accomplished without your ever being aware of it, and merely waits for your readiness. Events are being arranged everywhere, and your willingness to proceed will open your eyes to the eventful.

Try to become aware that only outside of your intent is the illusion of the ego, telling you that your desires, or mission, if you will, are impossible. But because of your awareness of the truthfulness and sincerity of this intent within you, the outside is clearly only a means for time to tick on by, and you'll easily be able to overlook it. By looking beyond time, you'll see the Holy Spirit's need for using it to support your efforts. Allow Him to be your "Teacher in time" for your benefit, which benefits humanity as a whole. It's the groundwork being laid out for you.

Chapter 23
Healing in Order to Forget

As you look back on your life you may notice points where you think some groundwork was laid for you, and that you might have missed out. Or maybe you did see the welcome signs and you climbed aboard with your heart in what it had to offer you. Either way, you are where you are now for a reason that is meant to be.

To use myself as an example: All my life I had inner feelings and thoughts that in time had convinced me they were spiritual, but also controversial—beyond the religious dogma I was taught to believe in. Don't get me wrong. My youth gave me a strong foundation I'm thankful for. But what I was truly feeling was not endorsed by much of the world. Not until my early thirties would I be brave enough to begin expressing my thoughts, perceptions, and attitudes, by sharing them only with certain friends. I was ridiculed as foolish.

I was still uncertain and plagued with questions I could not get answers to, leaving myself hopeless. But one thing for certain: my unconventional thinking was growing, and it was flowing from an inspiration I knew was real and true, regardless of what the world was telling me. I did not doubt this voice that urged my sprouting thoughts.

I began to browse the self-help section in bookstores. As I researched and read the ideas of authors who had already been where I was, and had broken through their own fears, I found they all had one common theme. They were excited and elated about their discovery, and they wanted to pass along their views to seekers like me, with no strings attached. A good example is Wayne W. Dyer, who wrote a book called *Pulling Your Own Strings*—a concept I was able to tap into.

Some of the authors I agreed with, and many I did not. Of the ones I agreed with, I often noticed they would occasionally refer to a publication with which I was unfamiliar, called *A Course in Miracles*. Each time I would wonder, what is this *Course in Miracles*? However, with my hectic lifestyle and fast track as a "thirty-something," I never seemed to take the time to investigate what this spiritual subject matter called *A Course in Miracles* was all about. I always intended to look further, but I never did. As it happens, it was totally unlike me to procrastinate on anything, but for some unknown reason I continued to put it off as a "one of these days" type of reminder to myself.

Several years later I made the wrong-minded choices that eventually sent me to prison, where of all places, during my despair and turmoil, and at age fifty, I literally stumbled into *A Course in Miracles*. Keep in mind that in prison there are holy books and religious material, such as the Bible, lying around everywhere. But since I have been in prison I have not yet, to this day, seen another single copy of the *Course*.

After my unexpected and unsearched-for "find" of this Godsend, I discreetly asked other inmates, as well as prison employees, including a librarian, if they had ever heard of *ACIM*, and their answers have always been a quick "No." But the librarian did offer a comment after she replied, "A course in *what*?" She went on to add sarcastically that "a miracle was not going to release me from prison." My mission was to prove otherwise.

Confused and Curious

Was this series of abstract material destined to find me? If so, why in prison? The answers to these questions and more are no longer a mystery to me. But its presence did find me and has opened my mind to a whole new world, the real world.

I am continually learning that there is really nothing for me to fear. Now I am sharing my thoughts and views by extending the truth about who and what I am, as I continue to learn. There are many people in the world today who are as confused and curious as I once was, who want to feel secure in looking beyond the body, but are afraid to do so. Is this the Holy Spirit's use of time with me, as well as a good example of His undoing of my errors and the arranging of events? It certainly is, and no one could know this but me.

But let's look at this more closely. There is no doubt in my mind that throughout the years of my life I was certainly being led, not necessarily to *A Course in Miracles*, but to a spiritual reality I could feel united with. The *Course* is simply the tool the Holy Spirit used, based on my state of readiness to clearly see beyond the body.

I have described the event of my greeting *ACIM* in detail in my first book, *The Master of Everything*, which I consider to be the pilot book for the material you hold in your hands now. But was I supposed to go to prison in order for this to occur? No, not at all. At that time, though, with all that was going on in my life before being sent to prison, it was the Holy Spirit's best method for getting my attention. My "house built on sand" needed to be leveled and rebuilt on a "foundation of solid rock."

Did the Holy Spirit bring on the events that led me to prison? Of course not; the ego in me did. But the Holy Spirit used my errors to get me *ready* and *willing* for a long-overdue change. He saw prison as the perfect opportunity.

Since the construction began on my new house built on rock, I have been able to forget the past by forgiving myself and move forward along the path that is being arranged for me. No one can sincerely forgive (look beyond) and not be healed where inner peace is the gift. But let's not confuse looking beyond with looking to the future, because the future is another ego fantasy.

To be healed is to forget the past so you can remember who you are. No one can make a hell and think it is real, nor can he make a dream become true. Many have said that they do practice forgiving others and themselves, but few really have knowledge of its meaning; therefore, forgiveness never gets the chance to truly prevail. Their idea of forgiveness is false, and stagnates as illusion. This world will take on a different image, should at least two minds agree that peace is the only life they *want* to live.

The Only True Answer

Why would we run around looking for all sorts of answers other than the one that will answer everything for all time to come? It's peace that we truly want. Peace is the perfect answer given to imperfect questions, meaningless requests, and half-hearted desires. To forgive is all there need be, which is to see yourself in reality, which is beyond ego-based thought. If you let go of the ego, all that remains is your true reality.

Of course I'm not saying that you should not protect yourself, or not call the authorities if someone is out to harm you. Even when we must protect ourselves, our own forgiveness practice must remain to be the "looking beyond" of someone else's errors in thought. When faced with a difficult situation with another person, ask yourself, "What is beyond his actions?"

What if we all looked beyond the ego's methods of gaining and winning, where others must lose? If we all overlooked ego-based behavior by looking beyond it, would this mean we could begin living beyond it? Yes, of course! I hope you can now see why I am so excited and pleased. All along previously in my life, the ego had been teaching me that "What is beyond is delusional"—but since then I have been able to uncover and expose the ego for the emptiness and void that it truly is.

God has a plan for salvation that cannot fail, and I'm not speaking of "rising from the dead." I am speaking of you having the power to multiply "fish and loaves" for the good of humankind, simply by living your true free will. This is His Plan for salvation.

Be grateful and "take the bull by the horns," so to speak, so you can live a life that reflects what you *want*. Don't be afraid. The bull and its horns are not real, so you can't be harmed. Anything opposite of what you *want* is illusion. Without changing God's Plan for you, it stands before you, waiting. This message has been in humanity's mind for centuries, but most have missed its true meaning.

Chapter 24
An Exercise for Peace of Mind and Certainty

By continuing to look outside yourself, you are simply delaying your free will. You can forgive your past, as I have done, and let it go, by looking beyond to where you begin to give as you receive at the same time. Unlike what the ego would have you believe, there is no plan for salvation, other than this. The ego has had us all searching for fantasy. Let it go and forgive yourself. It's okay; you can now forget and look beyond deceit and doubt, by keeping it simple.

Try to see that all complexities of the world are behind you now. When doubt, indecisiveness, confusion, or many of the other struggles we face seem to get you down, you need a solid way to stop fooling yourself about your own uncertainties.

Many of us have taught ourselves the unnatural habit of an untrue method for communicating with God, who is the Source, or Lamp, if you will, that our light forever shines from. We're of Him, and we remain in close communication with ourselves, yet we have been fooling ourselves by looking outside of who we are when trying to get in touch with God. We seem to try sending "out" our prayers.

We squint our eyes, or close them, and think hard as we try to push brain energy outward so that God may receive our requests. But we're missing the mark. Everything of God is already in us. We must unlearn the idea of separateness and learn of the happy communication that is not only what we are capable of, but is our power. It can't be lost.

Whenever you are in doubt or troubled about what you should do, simply make a request to the truth in you, the Holy Spirit, who abides in your right-mind. With all sincerity, simply ask:

Decide for me.

Then consider it done with confidence, but not boastfulness. Be humble by knowing His decisions are the reflections of what God knows about you, and any error in this decision is impossible.

Why would you frantically struggle to anticipate all you cannot know, when all knowledge lies behind every decision the Holy Spirit makes for you? Learn of His

Wisdom and Love that rests within you, and *trust* in the decision you'll be making. Additionally, in your own unique style, discreetly, respectfully, and with care, tenderly teach His Answer to others who struggle as you have. Your own true story is often a good lesson to share, as I have shared mine with you. You must be yourself.

Going beyond All Words

Here is a meditation technique that I prefer to use that helps me to go beyond all words and physical form seen as special. Feel free to use these words in prayer if this is more comfortable for you. What we want to attempt, this time, is to reach a quickened place on a shorter path to a peace of mind you desire and deserve. Simply close your eyes and forget all that you thought you knew and understood.

While using your own proven breathing style for meditating, and as you sink into your desired state of mind and of physical relaxation, repeat the following words:

> I am not a body.
> I'm free and I'm as God created me.
> I have a function He wants me to fill.
> I'm aware it can only be my true free will.

Understand that it will be normal to have idle thoughts; try to permit none of them to go unchallenged. If you notice one, deny its hold and hasten to assure your mind that this is not what you want. In other words, let go of these idle thoughts. Do this by gently letting the thought you denied to be given up, in a sure exchange for an idea that enforces your meditation.

You can go about this by using the following formula as you say to yourself:

This thought I do not want. I choose instead . . .
(Then insert one, or each, of the following)

> . . . to find the function that would set me free from all the illusions of this world.

or

> . . . to remember that the past is gone, the future is not yet. Now I am freed from both.

or

> . . . to stay not an instant longer where I don't belong.

Allow me now to share an example of how I will use this practice when I feel my past errors that landed me in prison haunting and hounding me, which I must admit does try to take its toll on me. I am able to rescue myself from these nasty thoughts by saying the following words during my meditation. Also, I will never rule out a short prayer when my state is not conducive to meditation.

> Holy Spirit, I trust you as my Guide and I'm having some thoughts I don't want. These thoughts bind me this morning, and I'm having trouble letting go of them. I choose to remember instead that the past is gone and the future is not yet here. Now that I have remembered this, I know I am now freed from both past and future.

Become comfortable with this, and develop a style that is right for you. Any one of these statements will be enough to subdue your idle, wrong-minded thoughts, plus it will add strength to the sincerity of your prayers. This should be done quickly, and trust that great effort or strain is not necessary. In fact, trying too hard will give the ego a chance to haunt you further. There's no need to turn this into some kind of lengthy or arduous ritual.

Once you feel that the distracting, idle thoughts have left you, go back to the original meditation, and do not worry about further idle thoughts coming along. If they do, simply repeat the exercise, and with time and practice these pesty thoughts will diminish, becoming less persistent and less frequent. The meditation will become stronger for you, and with a power the ego will eventually get tired of trying to disrupt.

PART IV
THE POWER
OF YOUR HEALING MIND

Chapter 25
The Unhealed Healer

Around the same time my troubles in life were getting ready to send me to prison, I didn't find it too strange that suddenly I would become a fan of the late singer and songwriter Johnny Cash. It was his own rough times, as portrayed in the motion picture *Walk the Line* about portions of his life, that sent me rushing out to buy a few of his music CDs. I can still hear his rugged voice expressing his views of the world.

Here in prison my main source of news from the outside world is my trusted pocket-sized radio. I can often be seen with headphones circled around my head, listening to my favorite talk shows, news, and music stations. This is one of the ways to escape the extreme loudness, vulgarity, crudeness, and chaos that contributes to the madness of the prison environment. Having a radio is a blessing that must be self-guarded due to ongoing theft of personal property.

One day, when a rough morning had just ended for me, while lying on my back on my bunk and scanning the radio stations, I discovered an interview with singer and songwriter Rosanne Cash, the daughter of legendary Johnny Cash. Her message touched me. It was a lesson for me and for my own journey that came from her open heart and mind.

Rosanne began to discuss at length how, early in her career, she struggled with songwriting. She couldn't seem to be consistent in the direction she wanted her career to take her. She felt as though she was obligated not only to protect, but also follow the image and level of success the world had projected for her father. She knew she had much of her own reality she wanted to extend. Only when Rosanne Cash was able to let go of two things was she able to write music from her own heart, with lyrics that were screaming to be revealed.

First of all, she had to let go of what the world expected of her. Next, she had to put away the seeming magic wand she was given for success, which was being the protégé of her world-famous father. Once she was able to decide to get rid of both, she was able to settle down within herself as a true professional in her own way.

This lovely and friendly woman, proud of her late father and his accomplishments, recalled her own first sold-out solo concert. Rosanne described how terribly nervous and frightened she was during the entire show. The talk show host Diane Rehm, on WNPR, was able to pull the words out of her guest, so that this particular interview, in which Rosanne Cash recalled her first concert, became another step through a doorway to helping others overcome stage fright for many of life's occasions where we must perform.

Rosanne said her father helped by giving her some words of wisdom based on his own experiences on center stage. "Just keep showing up," he always insisted to her. Rosanne went on to say that nervousness and uncertainty seem to always exist at some level, even if very minor. But while still nervous, the "showing up," she says, remains a continuous thrill, because she always shows up as she truly is, and not as a shadow figure of her father, Johnny Cash.

Today she looks back on these struggles, and the current ones as well, as not really being struggles at all, but merely more of not knowing how to handle the effects of time restraints. She said that now all these hassles are not seen as real hassles, and have no role in limiting herself. Whatever problems pop up, her faith in her own real self allows her to deal with things easily.

I was deeply impressed with this interview with Rosanne Cash, which I found honest, upfront, and down to earth. It more than made my day. She concluded the show by adding that she no longer allows such anxiety to get the best of her; on the contrary, she now sees any such nervousness as teaching her that healing in some form is taking place—a healing in order to grow. Rosanne looks at everything she went through as being necessary to bring out the joy she now hands down to her own children. Her music today is a thrill for me to listen to, and gives me a gift of calmness when I think about my own direction.

No One Heals on His Own

There's no doubting the fact that musicians like Rosanne Cash and her late father Johnny write beautiful songs that penetrate us somehow. The feelings we get from such an art are intrinsic and are not physical, but our bodies do go along for the joy ride. Is it the musicians' bodies that create this joy?

No, it's not, and just as the body is merely the instrument that houses the ability while it is communicated, we are not limited to the body. These abilities are simply decisions the Holy Spirit helps us make deep within the mind, where He abides as an aspect of who we actually are. God communicates this to us through the Holy Spirit, which is universally in us all. This oneness of mind is what gives us truth in the decisions we make, which gives us sincerity.

Although the body can be a messenger, it can only be the mind that creates the thought to be communicated. It is the mind that instructs the brain (the body) to begin its message-sending. But it is possible that the mind may get lost, or even arrested inside the brain, due to a belief that nothing is beyond the body. This is when wrong-mindedness prevails, with confusion, chaos, and other fearful feelings.

This can make the ego a hard shell to crack. But you don't have to "crack" it. You can choose to let go of the ego easily, because it is unaware that it has no chance to eliminate your willingness to do so. The whole mind has an ongoing willingness to create, and the ego continues to go out of its way to try and prove to you it doesn't need wholeness and that a separate identity is safer.

This is where our perceptions play their hand as a stepping stone, either up to knowledge or down to ignorance. When you operate from the whole mind, you don't need to derive a sense of safety by following the crowd, because you're real enough to "walk the line" of your own chosen destiny.

Of course the ego will try to convince you that the body already does act on its own and is self-sufficient. But the belief in self-sufficiency— separateness—is a wrong-minded attitude that makes for a behavior pattern and mental state not suited for learning, nor for teaching. Remember, beliefs are what you make yourself, then erroneously call truths.

Does Truth Need a Belief?

The dream of separation from the Mind of God was the beginning of belief systems, which have grown and fragmented from one generation to the next. We can say that once we began believing, the first tick of time was initiated. We began believing that it was actually morning, afternoon, and evening. Someone had to give us a valid reason for believing there should be noon, to separate out the morning, and likewise for having a belief there should be a *mid-night*.

We began believing in a time to get old, a time to attack, a time to blame, to feel guilty; then it became a time to pray, a time to repent. Did we make this time from our beliefs, or was it created? What would a fish say if we could ask it, "What time is the best time for you to swim?" If the fish was being truthful, it would say "Now." Now is the only real time there is.

Please consider, why would the unseparated mind, which is one with its Creator, ever have the need for a single belief? When you have everything and are lacking nothing, you don't need to believe in anything. But perhaps you will say that you do lack, and that you do not have everything. Are you certain of this?

Ask yourself: Does real, honest truth ask you to believe in it as a reinforcement? No, it does not, and it does not need your belief in it to make it true. What is true, is true, regardless of how many beliefs support it. Our knowledge of it is enough. So why is it we feel the need to believe in anything?

We are all teachers at some level, even if you are the only student. Couldn't we then say that to teach from our beliefs would weaken us as teachers and as learners? Nonetheless, we continue to teach what we believe, and what others have taught us to believe in, and then we consider the lesson learned as knowledge.

Our behaviors change alongside our beliefs, and this results in inconsistent learning patterns, making us poor teachers and poor learners. In this state we are unable to heal and continue along in the dream of life as fantasy, and live it as unhealed healers. If we teach both separateness and healing, then we are simply sowing more of this conflict. The more we separate, the more we struggle with healing.

Anytime a mind is split it requires a lesson in healing, to keep it from continuing to split. As it continues to fragment it still senses the light of right-mindedness, although some areas of the fragmenting mind are more obscured from the light than the rest. We must look to our right-mindedness as the Light of the Holy Spirit, our Teacher, Communicator, and Healer.

Healing and Magic

As the Holy Spirit uses the body constantly for communication purposes, we must understand its connection with healing. No one has healing abilities of his own, and anyone who considers himself "a healer" doesn't understand this—is an unhealed healer.

In order that the fragmenting aspect of the mind that believes in separateness, called the ego, can be healed, we must have the ability—the availability—to heal. The Holy Spirit's role in the world works through this innate ability that we all have. He doesn't recognize anything else where the ego is concerned, only healing of the split-mind. He has nothing to do with the ego's confusion over mind and body.

Remember, because of humanity's decision to fantasize of a separate mind, the ego and the Holy Spirit are within us, except one is real and the other is the illusion that dreams. Anything unreal cannot be of God; therefore, why should you fear "anything?"

I realize this all sounds great about not having to be fearful. But think about this further. A mind can communicate, but can it actually harm you? The body as ordered by the ego can harm itself, as well as other bodies. But this will never occur unless the body has already been confused with the mind. In other words, by having an unconfused mind, you'll have no worries of harm, or of "anything," for that matter. The mind wouldn't even think about harm; therefore, all conflict too should not be a concern.

When it comes to healing, the error occurs in the ego's convincing us that it is self-sufficient. Think deeply here about what really happens to you when you are healing from any type of illness or injury. Isn't the process to healing strengthening you? Of course it is. But the ego prefers to believe that healing is a painful process and comes from outside—that something or someone outside us heals us; that it occurs through magic. This is an insane belief by which we operate, and this is why we have so many types of "magic" pills and formulas.

Magic is always seen as something fabulous or wonderful in the healer. He believes he can offer something as a gift to someone who does not have it. He may believe that the gift was sent from God to him, and in turn, as a healer, he passes it along to you. But he doesn't understand God if he believes he has something that others lack.

Chapter 26
Healing and Harmony

When the Holy Spirit heals it is not random; it is due to favoritism. Yes, that's right, He favors you because He is you. He is the aspect of yourself that rules over your right-minded thoughts leading to perceptions, which ultimately shift forward to knowledge.

Time certainly is involved, and the substance of knowledge needed determines the amount of time the Holy Spirit will use. Thinking you can heal yourself without His steadfastness and changelessness makes you an unhealed healer, giving you confusion over your thoughts, which will give you trouble seeing results. Healing must be conflict-free and is necessary for wholeness.

By making exceptions and acknowledging that you can sometimes heal yourself, and other times not, you place yourself into conflict and inconsistency. This will cause you to start forming beliefs about yourself. It might be of a few famous words of wisdom, or well-meaning but misinformed sentiments passed along to us by the world in an effort to help us build self-esteem. Or old adages said by an ancestor in your family who you believe was wise only because they lived a long life.

These so-called esteeming type messages we instill in our children, just as they were instilled in us, such as my favorite—one I've heard over and over: "You can do anything you wish if you put your heart into it." If this is true, we might want to consider where it is our hearts truly are, or where they have been all along.

Why should I have to place my heart somewhere? "My heart is (or is not) where I want it to be" is a thought that always struck me. How many times have you thought or said to yourself, "I'm not willing to put my heart into this?" Was it because you didn't believe strongly enough? Truly, how hard must you believe in order to place your heart somewhere other than where your heart already is?

If you can answer these questions truthfully within yourself, then you will know where your heart sincerely is, or is not. It may only be for the time being that you discover the only place your heart truly is, is at a place that knows it is not where you thought it was. How truthful is this?

Getting Turned Around

A Course in Miracles teaches us, "What is of God is for all things, because all that is real is wholly of God."

This must tell us that since the love we have within us is real, and therefore must be of God, then this love must not have a single exception. What I mean here is that we make up our own exceptions, just as we make up our own beliefs. So really, then, what's the difference between an exception and a belief?

Don't we think we need them both, to protect us from, or to cover up, our fears? They both are used as a weapon for defense. "This is my belief, so I must stick with it at all costs" is a statement we will use that seems to justify a stance taken during conflict. How then can we heal ourselves when we carry this conflict, and how can our perceptions be meaningful?

The fear that has been fostered by this conflict cannot possibly bring you joy, whereas healing does, and peace comes with it. Think of the peace you feel when you know you're healing from any given problem. Healing is consistent by the Holy Spirit and involves His constant undoing of errors. Rather than asking Him to heal you by fixing a situation or circumstance in your life that is giving you difficulty, ask that He help you to understand how healing is taking place.

Ask that He help you to first perceive, and then to know, what to do. This could happen immediately, all at once, or there could be a period of time between perceiving and actually knowing what to do, or even in knowing that you are on the healing path.

Ask, too, that you become aware of His Guidance. If you act on a perception that seems solid, but are mistaken, don't worry; it's okay. He will use this mistake as a step toward a higher perception if necessary, or on to knowledge. As long as you sense His ever-prevailing Guidance, you cannot be off track. It may seem that you are stuck in one place, but this is only temporary. The Holy Spirit uses time to get you moving in the right-minded direction. But sometimes He must abruptly stop you in your wrong-minded tracks, and then turn you around.

Your Reflection of the World

Perception does not yield; it is more like looking into a mirror. What you see and how you view things is a reflection of your inner state of mind. There is no doubt in my mind that I am experiencing being turned around at this time of my life while in prison.

Being stuck in jail for the time being, my mind heals while I share what I continue to learn with my open heart. I hear the voice, a strong thought, an urging if you will, instructing me to write while events are being arranged to carry out the necessary tasks to get this book into your hands, so this message may be received. This, as well as my release from prison, will take place in due time. I'm being taught by my Teacher to relax without fear, and everything will be fine.

I have come to know my Teacher intimately, which is the Holy Spirit in my mind. My real *Self*. His guidance and lessons are everywhere, and teach me in more ways all the time what it is I should do next. I am seeing that each step I take is instructed to me carefully and slowly, because of His chosen use of time.

Already, through a friend who came out of my past to help, I've been put in contact with a professional literary editor, whom he'd sought out for me. Her name is Carol, living in Florida, and she keeps me realistic in my goals. We've been communicating through regular U.S. mail only, the basic method of communication for a prisoner, since computer access is unauthorized. All I can say in these beginning stages of working well with her is that things look extremely positive. I'm able to trust in her own right-mindedness. As with anything else, time will tell.

The Holy Spirit is using the fact and the experience of my incarceration as a whole, to set my mind in an inspired motion that I would not ordinarily have had as a free man. Why? Prison seems to have given me no other *real* choice. However, the signs are everywhere that my release early from prison is not too far off.

I see the littlest of events unfolding around me indicating my freedom. I hear His voice, or thought, calmly suggesting when I should write and when I should read. Here in prison, with mass overcrowding, writing space, such as a spot at a table or a countertop, is difficult to come by. Often I stand at my top bunk, using it as a desktop. But lately I seem to have had fewer problems finding a corner or end of a table with just enough space to bring out my pen and composition journal. Often it's while a card game is going on. In fact, some of the other inmates seem to look out for me while not asking questions, which is odd. It's as though they sense the importance of the work, due to the calm seriousness of my demeanor. There are those who ridicule me behind my back, but I ignore it.

Showing Up

The Little Garden Society, at first seemingly and then later certainly, began showing its presence to me. I was seeing myself consistently continuing to "show up," as the Cash family—Johnny through his daughter Rosanne—had suggested on the Diane Rehm radio talk show, which I described earlier. And there was Reese Witherspoon's interview, which found me in order to inject a jolt of inspiration at the perfect time. Ironically, she portrayed Johnny Cash's wife, June Carter, in the movie *Walk the Line*.

I do realize that it may seem ridiculous for me to deem these individuals a part of the secret society for "endurance and inspiration." But at least for now, please withhold judgment and continue to read on. Others will be popping up along the way, like a "pop-up" on your computer, and a welcome one at that.

On another day when thoughts were urging positivity inside me, it hit me to write a letter to the Foundation for Inner Peace, the copyright holder of *A Course in Miracles*. The thought had been in the back of my mind for some time that ultimately I would need permission to quote particular passages from its content. Something suggested I do so this particular day so I could see what type of response, if any, I might receive. Naturally I had no experience in such matters.

Less than two weeks later I received a reply letter from the foundation. Not only were they giving me a green light to continue with my mission, they encouraged me as well. The kind letter expressed appreciation and was signed by a woman who I could tell was extremely knowledgeable about the *Course*. I do not mention her name here because I did not obtain her permission to do so, though I remain grateful to her.

In her letter she expressed an understanding of my situation in prison, along with my desire to secure a publisher that was right for my material. She complimented my perseverance, but openly admitted she was in no position to recommend a publisher. This made perfect sense to me, since *A Course in Miracles* recognizes itself as "esoteric" in nature and it would be counter to this quality were it to favor certain publishers or other such referrals.

I received her letter at a time when I had been struggling over a particular section in the book you're reading now. However, a simple but meaningful sentence she used in closing her letter triggered a series of thoughts that were *ready*, due to my *willingness*, to come forward in my mind. I immediately jotted everything down in the little research notepad I carry around in my hip pocket. I've learned to always be ready for an unexpected set of words that need to be noted. After a full day of sitting with her words, I was able to abundantly expand on her gift to me, which allowed me to freely complete that section of this book.

Since the woman's letter I have received honest and helpful words from others, but no one has indicated that they received my name, address, and situation from her. I don't really have a clue otherwise how some have gotten in touch with me, other than by word of mouth. Some have given me a source, but they can't tell me how their source was able to pass along my contact information.

A postcard showed up from a retired literary agent, Barb, typed on an old-fashioned typewriter with a worn key. This, she said, was her style when writing to friends. But how did I suddenly become her friend? I can't answer that. My guess is that she was somehow connected to a writing correspondence course I once enrolled in. Also odd was that I only heard from her once, with no return address on the postcard. I believe she lives in Colorado, as she briefly described the beauty of the Rocky Mountains, and she wrote that she is "with me in spirit."

She added that her business connections had dwindled since her retirement, but she did lead me to a resource directory that would possibly help me obtain a publisher for my books. She warned me of the uphill climb I was facing and encouraged me to continue. No frills or thrills. That was it. But somehow her postcard itself was my thrill. I use it as a bookmarker in my copy of the *Course*.

Another letter showed up from a romance novelist named Susan, urging me to keep my pen in hand, along with other inspiring words. She added that I should not "wait for the ink to dry." I took this as encouragement to keep moving forward, never stopping. All she could tell me further was that she had run into an old friend of mine while out to lunch on a Sunday afternoon. I never found out who it was.

Joel, a man who plays the cello in a symphony orchestra, has written me several letters, giving me insight on how to pick out the cello among all the instruments during a performance. Now, when I listen to the all-night classical music station on my radio, I can easily bring to mind the cello line. This new skill adds something a bit ethereal to my listening pleasure. There are many late nights or wee morning hours when I'll listen to classical music that soothes me. For this new understanding of each instrument in the orchestra, I have Joel to thank. Later during the course of our correspondence, he did confess that he had been given my contact information by his church in New York City—though I don't know how it got there, and I don't know anyone in New York. He and his wife live in Manhattan but go to church on Staten Island. I was born at an army hospital on Staten Island in 1957. Just a coincidence?

The most exciting letters I've received, and I will explain why in more detail later on, are from a woman in Croatia, Nakita, who offered me tremendous inspiration. She told me of a man from the United States she once met while he was visiting her country on a concert tour. He sang and played guitar professionally. She went on to tell me that she had heard him perform at an area concert for world peace, and that he was on a similar spiritual path as myself. Through friends of hers, she was able to meet this musician and spend some quality time together. During their discussions she discovered his passion for the lessons and principles contained in *A Course in Miracles*. Her encouragement for me to keep the faith and all that "stuff" has proven to be successful.

Deeply Seeing Others

It wasn't until a woman and her husband, neither of whom I have met, sent me a card with a letter enclosed did I truly begin to see the deep and true side in all of us. The husband is a Protestant minister and pastor of his own church. He didn't mention the affiliation because he noted to me that it wasn't necessary.

The couple is from the Gulf Coast area of Louisiana, where the tragic BP oil spill had wiped out the fishing industry. The minister and his wife were heavily involved in doing all that they could to help the fine folks in that area who suffered loss as a result. This was the only correspondence I received from them, and its purpose was mostly to let me know I was in their prayers and in the prayers of the members of their church.

The healing we experience does bring harmony to the spirit, to our attitude, and in turn increases the love and inner peace we're willing to extend, even when we're in a bad situation, like I am here in this hostile prison environment. Every day for me is more than a test of my sanity. But I sense a belonging to something pure and powerful, and this keeps me motivated in truth.

I'm experiencing the wholeness of the Holy Spirit's healing effects. Yes, I am consciously aware of the separateness within myself healing. I'm able to count on these effects because the *Cause* is God. It is real, and being of God, the Holy Spirit is keeping me inspired.

I feel a consistency in my mind's healing process, especially when I'm writing. The words seem to arrive when I need them the most, and when I'm researching any particular area a resource becomes available. The more I write, the more the *Voice* tells me that I will be writing for many years to come, perhaps till I can no longer grip a pen or tap on a keyboard. Just as I finished writing these last few lines a smile came over me with a message. It told me to relax in confidence. In these secure sensations I have minimal conflict within myself.

At this time, as I write on this page in the composition journal, the State of Ohio, which holds me as a prisoner in one of its thirty-three teeming prisons, is experiencing the worst financial crisis in the state's history. All departments in the state, including the prison system, are forced to make drastic financial cuts.

Due to the state's past twenty-five-year "tough on crime" or "lock 'em up and throw away the key" stance, the prison system has become inhumanely and unconscionably, severely overcrowded. The prisons are at 138% capacity, and are a breeding ground for more than just disease. Sending a person to prison in Ohio has become big business. It has become an industry of which the general public is unaware. The prisons are nothing more than warehouses for more and more bodies than they can now afford to handle. Lots of federal dollars are involved, handed to the state to run its prisons, but the system is now far out of control and the funds are not enough for real rehabilitation—nor has rehabilitation ever been the goal or priority of the current "correctional" system.

The state's legislature has recently passed a prison reform bill, signed by Governor John Kasich, who I feel truly wants to do the right thing with sentencing disparity. The new reform bill will send fewer people to prison by using alternative rehabilitation measures. This new law also suggests a release from prison for many nonviolent crimes, like my own. This is great—but the sad but true fact is that it took a lack of money for the politicians and bureaucrats who run the state to finally recognize the problem. Their action is not the result of common sense or compassion, but of financial straits.

All in all, however, we can look at this as a shift from continuous error over to right-mindedness. The right-minded work of the Holy Spirit always prevails. In this case, can we see how He used the ego's lack in order that many see the light? For now, my instructions from Him tell me to wait, watch, listen, use my real vision, and keep on writing. It certainly lightens my load. It is healing.

Chapter 27
Knowledge Doesn't Depend on Beliefs

Healing involves a surrendering of yourself to what is real and truly meant to be. But you must understand and trust that what is not meant to be will ultimately be reversed, or undone. Consistent ongoings in physical form are part of this process.

There is something to be said for the statement "God works in mysterious ways." Since His meaning is changeless, so is each of ours. The trueness and the meaning about what or who we are is never out of accord with His, because our whole truthful meaning comes from His. Therefore, it must be like His. When we are unhealed we have doubts about this, which is why we become defensive about our beliefs.

One common belief seems to be: "I must defend myself if I am attacked." But *how* is it we believe we should defend ourselves? Surely we must defend against physical harm, but how do we *believe* we should go about this?

Let's not be too alarmed or hard on ourselves, because no one will be totally healed until as a whole we reach full Atonement. This is the Holy Spirit's goal with everything that occurs in this world, and why things occur the way they do. He has a use for everything. It would be foolish to say that God could ever be out of accord with Himself; therefore, how could you and I? It is the ego that separates us from all that God is.

Humankind is afraid to look deep within because we think we made ourselves a will—a will that is not true, but we made it seem to be real. In reality, this will humanity made has no effects; we cannot separate our real self from true reality, which is Christ, and is infinite and eternal. In other words, you cannot separate yourself from your Creator, not even in part. This oneness is infinite and has no separate parts. His infinite wholeness is you.

You may have doubts and serious mind-boggling questions as to yourself being Christ, and understandably so. This is because the ego in you places emphasis on a body and insists that Christ is separate from you. This is part of your dreaming mind that is carefully being healed, or awakened, based on your willingness and readiness, and on the given time in your life here on Earth while you dream.

It's as a whole that we are caught up in the dream of separate identities from that of God. But it's our individual healing that brings the whole to ourselves. This infinite realm of wholeness we call the Sonship is personalized as Christ. We're all an integral part of this vastness. But I anticipate the question: "Where is Jesus in all this?" He's right where He's always been as a Son of God, at Home, wholly joined with us.

Jesus, for only a short while, was God's Holy Spirit manifested in human form, who entered the dream as our elder brother to give certain lessons we may understand with the separated, dreaming mind. We must remember that what seems to us as some two thousand years ago, when Jesus walked and talked among many, was only a timeless instant ago in the reality of the unseparated, non-dreaming Self.

He projected that image for us to see, so we could relate from a fragmented mind's point of view, which cannot comprehend the timeless instant of the dream. The resurrection of Jesus, the man, was His example to us of total awakening from the dream, as the wholeness of Christ. Now He, as Christ, stands at time's end, guarding the Atonement process till we join Him as Christ.

For now, the Atonement is our true reality, and Jesus, as the Holy Spirit, while we dream, helps us to awaken. Am I saying that Jesus, the Holy Spirit, Christ, and God are the same and one? Yes, now you've got it! But don't miss out on seeing yourself in the Oneness as well.

The Beliefs You Make and Why You Make Them

As unhealed healers ourselves, the Atonement process itself urges us to begin to heal. However, healing problems start conflicting when you seek appreciation from your brother/sister, but do not appreciate him/her. This occurs when you think you are giving someone something and not receiving equally in return. The ego is thereby limiting your learning/healing.

This healing/learning is vital in its power for change, for when you recognize your own power for one instant, you can then change the world in the next. How so? Begin to understand that you are the world you see around you, because of the image you project from your perceptions of the world. So by changing your mind about what you see, you have changed the most powerful device that has ever been given you for change.

This is not contradictory to having a changeless mind as God created it; however, your ego *believes* you have changed it. This places you in a position to learn a lesson that seems to be contradictory. You must learn to change your mind about your mind. Only when you are willing to make this change will you see your own mind as changeless in reality.

In other words, be real. When you think you believe something to be true, like with eternity, sin, Heaven and hell, your relationship with God, or just about anything for that matter, honestly ask yourself the following question: *Why do I believe this?* Then ask: *What are my motivating factors here?* Next, move on to seeing your belief as one of the following: *Is it a thought or is it a perception? Or is it neither, and without a doubt is it pure, unmistakable knowledge?*

If your answer as the motivational factor is something like this: *I believe this way so that when I die I will join God in Heaven,* this would be a thought of something you wish to be true, and you call it a belief. But if it is a perception, your thought will have already made the belief, and now you're simply moving on to reinforce this belief by perceiving what you wish Heaven to be like. You will no longer have a need to make beliefs once you have accepted the knowledge within you. I mean what is truly in your heart.

Your own true "knowing" never changes, but beliefs do. Haven't we learned that God is changeless? In fact, your beliefs only keep you from attaining knowledge. Any and all knowledge you possess is totally absent of the ego, and this knowledge is who you are. Thoughts and perceptions always have some bodily influence, so be certain to accept them as such. When your perceptions do shift over to knowledge, however, they will do so naturally in time, without being forced by beliefs. Have you truly ever been able to force knowledge on yourself?

The Changeless You

When we are healing, we're learning how to be changeless. Don't get me wrong—physical appearances do change with time, and my fifty-five-year-old graying and thinning hair is proof enough of this. But I'm speaking of the "changeless you." As changes happen all around you in the physical world, the real you behind the separated, ego-based mind remains as you've forever been.

Only the ego in you changes—which is what? The false idea you believe yourself to be. I hope your knowledge can now see this with real vision, which is Christ vision. If you're not yet seeing this it's only because you haven't yet accepted it, which means you are not ready or willing to let go of the ego. But that's okay; we all come to this acceptance at our own rate. Once you are ready to let go of the ego, you'll also be able to recognize the changeless mind of others.

We all certainly know the truth within our own self, at our core, and we cannot fool ourselves the way we might fool others. The truth you do indeed know within yourself is who you are. So why hide from it? To help you along, just open up your right-mind, which consists of the appropriate thoughts and perceptions that encourage the Truth that is in you, so it can be seen for what you are.

Your ego doesn't understand anything about the right-mindedness you are capable of, however, because it doesn't understand the mind. So this can be difficult. Your ego may wish to think that this is nothing more than an attitude, rather than a mind.

If this is the case, then feel free to simplify the matter, and instead of right- or wrong-mindedness, call it right- and wrong-"attitudeness." It's all the same when it's true. Either way it's only a word, and its meaning is what is important. The meaning really comes from God anyway, and not from a dictionary. Being that it is of God means it's of the mind.

This is how you perceive the Holy Spirit in your brothers/sisters, through the right-mindedness of yourself and all others. It's the right-mindedness in your sisters/brothers that never changes the right-mindedness in you, until it shifts upward to the ultimate goal of One-mindedness. But even then it's really not a change. It's total union. Try to see that by changing your mind about him/her, you help undo the change their ego thinks it has made in them—the belief in separation. Your projections are what you see in your brother/sister. In other words, you choose what you decide to see.

One way you can accomplish this goal is by not responding to attack thoughts. By having an attitude that shows you have no need for defense or defensive thinking, you have changed his mind about his way of thinking, or "attitude."

If it is a difficult situation and a reply is necessary, your response could be something along the lines of: "Is that so?"—as a sincere question, not a challenge. Or, if you are expected to give a clear answer to an irate question, and the pressure is on you to do so, simply say: "At this time I truly don't know how to answer this." You have kept Truth involved without insulting anyone. Then let it be and see it as now past, as something you are done with.

Your Knowledge Is of Him

Remember, the purpose of this book is to help you consider that your mind is inside of the infinite Mind of God. So while you dream of being separate from His Mind, you are hearing two voices that make you see in two different ways.

One way shows you an image, or an idol, that you have learned to worship out of fear, but can never truly love. How can you love what you fear? The other way shows you only Truth. This you certainly love, and it brings you joy because you understand it as who you are. You don't have to "believe" it because you "know" its stability, and the truth in its peace. This is why you understand it.

If you're having some conflict over this, consider, for example, forming a private attitude, as I have learned from my good friend William Schenk: *"This is what I was told. This is what my own truthful views are. These ideas of someone else, along with my own, I will take under advisement within myself."*

This is a great attitude. Then you can ask your Teacher to sort this out for you, which He has already done. Bring it forward in your mind. Then you can relax while the process naturally begins. Any beliefs you try to manufacture one way or the other will only disturb or delay the naturalness of the lesson.

Understanding is merely appreciating the knowledge we can identify with, as a part of who we are, while accepting it with love. When you truly understand *why* your spouse, child, friend, or coworker might be upset, this is a loving response in your mind, even when you don't mention it. Words do not need to be exchanged.

God created us within His Mind in understanding and love, so this is what we are. The ego is unable to understand this—since there is no conflict—and thus cannot appreciate it. If you were to respond negatively to your upset spouse, this would feed the ego's hunger for conflict.

The ego in each of us always wishes to deprive someone of something, even if it's within yourself, so it can feel it has increased itself or its own worth or value in some way. But Heaven, if you will, rests in your giving of it, and as you give it, so does it increase.

With your understanding of this, do you want to give joy and have inner peace, or do you wish to remain in conflict? Conflict at its best can only one day fade away into dust along with its body, but your real mind is eternal. This is why Jesus once said, "Come therefore unto me, and learn of the Truth (Christ-Mind) in you." Jesus had the knowledge (not a belief) that Christ is in each of us, where we unite by bringing about joy.

Chapter 28
Are You Making or Creating Your Life?

How can anyone be partly angry? Does a smaller attack give it less meaning and make it less volatile? When we are angry in any degree, I'm sure you'll agree, it is still anger.

We love the idea of making wholeness, so we piece together fragments as if a puzzle, in a seeming effort to gain wholeness. Our intentions are good. This is how we can believe we are only a little bit angry, as though we're preserving the rest of ourselves as maintaining our good intentions.

Regardless of the size of our anger, though, attack is attack, and whether physical, verbal, or in thought, we must let go of it entirely. Fear and love are what either make or create. We *make* lives for ourselves out of the fear of being nothing or having nothing. Or we make a life by only getting by, surviving. But we *create* out of love, regardless of what we have.

This will depend on whether the ego is *begetting*, or the Holy Spirit is *inspiring*. The ego begets, or fathers itself, by denying wholeness. This is why the ego-based mind interprets "God gave His only begotten Son so that He may save the world" as a sacrifice or a loss. But the Holy Spirit doesn't see it this way, through Christ vision. His interpretation of "begotten Son" means fatherhood by wholeness, so that we, ourselves, may awaken as His only Son in wholeness, just as we were created. An awakening of all individual minds, including the mind of Jesus, as one mind, not a body, following Jesus out of the dream of separation: This is what will save the world.

As you contemplate the Truth in this, also see that a loving mind cannot accept attack, because the thought was never created. It's not a real thought, only a dream thought. The mind that accepts attack cannot love and wishes to destroy love, only because it doesn't understand it. What it does not understand, it fears. Therefore, not understanding love, it can't perceive itself as loving. It only dreams about love—a fantasy.

This, of course, is the part of each one of us that is illusory. This is a belief that there's nothing to be other than a body, which is not capable of love. Such a belief leads you to confusion with no sense of what is real or unreal.

Your thoughts may lead you to the body because of the power involved—the powerful pull of the ego, which identifies with the physical. But your thoughts may save you from this as well, because the power of real thoughts is not of the body's making. Try to remember that the ego mind *makes*, whereas the reality of God *creates*. Which have you been operating from?

As a true being of the reality of God, you have the ability to direct your thoughts as you choose. If you don't know that you do, then you must begin perceiving this as so. Within time this perception will transform—shifting into the knowledge you've been denying yourself. This is the power you have within your own thoughts.

Once you begin accepting this fact, you will begin *knowing* that you made beliefs about your mind being powerless. You will begin noticing that you've been holding yourself back by denying yourself, and by doing so you have been delaying your part in the Atonement, where it is needed. The world needs you.

Do you see the illusion we make of ourselves? It's called ego, and it's brilliant at preserving itself by attacking what it is preserving. We do this all the time when we see ourselves as "not rich enough" or "not smart enough" or "not strong enough," and on and on. The list continues with the endless ways we attack ourselves, bringing on anxiety from raised doubt, thus *making* more fear.

The real you cannot create fear, because God knows nothing of fear. The ego has made the mold for it. This is why the ego never recognizes what it's really doing. The ego draws from the one source that is totally averse to its existence, so that it may continue to exist. It leeches itself onto your Wholeness and then makes fantasy fragments of it, in order to make its own belief systems.

The Power of Your True Existence

The ego is afraid of your real power—the power deeply rooted in you, that "rock" about you, your true identity. The ego will try to avoid perceiving this power. It will work hard to depreciate your power with its wrong-minded thinking, leading to total wrong-mindedness. This type of thinking projects threat onto you, generating illusory perceptions that your inner realm is unreal. Thus the ego goes out of its way to believe Divinity, if it exists at all, is located someplace "out there."

This posture gives the ego a sort of assurance that your true Divineness is far away and will not interfere with its own thought system. The ego-based mind prides itself on the fact that its beliefs were built since time immemorial by generations of sacrifice.

The ego-based mind strives to gain paradise through continued sacrifice. In fact, if you do not buy into its fantasy, it will go to great lengths to convince you that you are in denial and living a life leaning toward sin through fantasy of your own. But there will come a point in time when the ego will tire of its convincing antics, when it sees its own life coming to an end. Meanwhile, you live on in peace, uninterrupted by illusory ego messages.

Your ego will also go out of its way to prevent any understanding about the true reality. Why? In response to its fear of the wholeness of knowledge, which is incapable of fragmenting or splitting apart. Instead, it makes beliefs in order to keep knowledge at a distance. Knowledge has no sizes or amounts or degrees; it is totally without division and certainly cannot be distanced.

Since the ego relies on what it believes, it doesn't have the capability to understand totality, let alone believe in it. This belief in fantasy is how it made itself through dreaming. It can never have a single concept of wholeness and is why a large part of us has a problem defining what is whole. The ego just cannot define it. Why? Because wholeness can't be made. This is why the ego's focus is always on its own projected image of yourself and of others, as only a body, and conversely, it sees anything else not of a body or material as fantasy, and a potential reason for being defensive.

Try to look a little deeper here, just for a moment or so, and see that the mind always produces as it was produced. In that seeming instant when the dream of separation initiated itself, the newly split-mind's own guilt produced fear, along with the ego-separated style of thinking. The ego-based mind has continued to produce fear ever since, through its fragmentation that it hopes will lend security.

To this day, in the same timeless dreaming instant, fear is its foundation, and makes it impossible for the ego to love anything. It can't even love itself, only because it is nothing. Who can love something that is unreal?

The ego-based mind in each of us will never realize that real love is the power of our true essence—which is why the ego denies it. But the part within us that senses pure joy from the power of love is Christ. When we operate from Christ, everything of our power flies directly over the ego's limited thinking, and this is why the ego can't love. All it can do is spend its energy trying to obscure our true light, by continuing to make fantasy until its bitter end.

Once you truly see that you—the real you, not your body—have everything and lack nothing, then you will never want to acknowledge the ego. You'll have no such "bitter end." In many cases in my own life now, this inspires me to stay clear of the views I once had of particular people, groups, and the world in general. The ego remains in all of us, until humanity as a whole reawakens. But my errors have been reflected upon, and I am able to realize the ego gradually fading away as I learn to silence it—for the most part. It's no longer my ego-based projections that make me tick.

Likewise, my ego now has difficulty attracting other egos. The Light about me is too bright for the ego to rule over my decisions. Is this an arrogant stance I take? Only to the ego. I am fully aware the ego is with me; otherwise, I wouldn't be in this body, the dream of projections. But my true light silences the ego, and with much joy I'm able to attract the realness and sincerity and fun-loving side in others. This is so even in prison, believe it or not. Sometimes, here in prison, all it takes with an angry inmate is for me to say something like this: "Come on, man. This prison thing is hell on all of us. Let's be real and help each other out." Their realness shines through.

The Little Garden Society operates by cultivating an awareness of the realness in others. We all have an illusory, ego-based side to ourselves, but as we progress this becomes more and more apparent. These days, the ego in another individual doesn't "waste its time" trying to lure me into conflict, so it may reel me in like a fish—as it could before. However, the true fun-loving, humorous, and sensitive, caring side of that same individual is the presence I relate to, and he has no thoughts of "going fishing" with "ego bait" when I am in his presence.

There is a down-to-earth side in everyone that *wants* to be shared. The Little Garden Society is able to spot this, leaving the ego at the door and seeing beyond it to the realness in an individual. For the most part, this is how humankind heals itself.

When we can interact this way, it is certain proof of the Holy Spirit communicating through each of us. This makes for a pleasant situation, especially for myself here in prison, where I can use all the "pleasantness" I can get, and then appreciate it like a bargain stock at an initial public offering (IPO), where the profits are shared. As I appreciate it, the extension is noticed, accepted, and then it appreciates even further. When it appreciates into your ego zone, this can be seen as the Whole seeking you out. When you, in turn, appreciate it, you've become whole.

Some situations with some individuals are more forward and others more timid, but in either respect on this scale, there might be more time needed for adjustment. How much time is up to the Holy Spirit. Any part of the Sonship that you display will be seen as whole. For instance, even a glimpse of joy or an instant of bliss is still joy as a whole. The ego will simply fade away, leaving only realness, which is all you could ever be.

Seeing Conflict as Meaningless

Being that you are the Sonship, that whole, lovable, giving and sharing and caring you, can you possibly see why the ego opposes and shies away from appreciation, all right-mindedness, and all real knowledge? When you see the love and good within yourself, this is the Sonship in you operated by the Christ-Mind. The ego will see only threat, judging you as arrogant, and will force itself to detach from you and attach itself quickly to anything else.

We see this frequently in relationships, when a couple breaks up. One or both of the parties rushes out to find a replacement. But sooner or later they find out that the "grass is not greener on the other side of the fence." The only reason the ego believes there is greener grass "out there" is because it made it up.

Immediately arrives the Holy Spirit to undo the illusion without attacking it—easily, because He doesn't perceive illusion at all. In fact, He never perceives anything, but rather knows. He knows exactly and precisely what you perceive as He mediates between truth and that of your dreaming mind. As the mediator, this is how He teaches you to perceive from a right-minded approach, or attitude. This is why you are then able to see a particular conflict as meaningless.

This is His method of resolving conflict through you, because He is you. Therefore, the next time you have resolved a conflict by seeing the simple senselessness of it, you have not only understood, but have witnessed, an *undoing* of error treated by your personal Healer. Or better yet, the Healer in you has prevailed as promised.

I hope you're seeing with real vision that the Holy Spirit is the Truth inside you. It's what created you, and this Truth is your knowledge. The Truth in you knows that conflict cannot be decided over "who did what to whom" or "who was at fault and who is to blame." Neither does the Truth in you want to dwell on "should have" or "would have" or "could have" done it differently. This is a pattern of fostering more beliefs. Rather, the Truth in you wants to understand that the reason you must let go of the conflict is because the conflict is meaningless.

You must release the conflict to Him. The Holy Spirit wants you to understand that conflict is not understandable, and thus all conflict is meaningless. Remember, it's what you choose to understand that brings on appreciation, and appreciation expands while extending love. But keep in mind, only Truth can be understood without conflict. What else is there?

Chapter 29
Accepting The Power of the Universe

Just like with your vegetable garden in the backyard, to live the most complete and whole life possible you must consider how you cultivate the soil of the garden. You must only allow natural fertilizers and nutrients to nourish its life. You truly cannot afford the infestation of wrong-mindedness taking root and spreading like weeds.

People who appear to be highly successful are no different from you or me. Ronald Reagan, when he was president, once made the comment that he was "no different than the other men in the world, who like himself, put their shoes on before their pants." No matter how we display a bit of humor, or dress ourselves in the morning, like everyone else we're an integral part of the same universal life Source. The Source is our power.

If you are able to bring to the front of your mind what the Holy Spirit has given you, then you will have minimal weeds and no obstruction to the growth of your garden. You'll no longer have the confusion over your beliefs in God, because you will *know* Him. You won't need beliefs.

If you like, change the name of God to suit your own reference within yourself—for example, "the Source of Life" or "the Strength of my own joy" or "the Power of the Real Universe." Whatever you choose, it's only a bundle of letters, and it's the meaning behind the letters we're after. Right? This simple change allows even the atheist or agnostic to see things more freely. Words alone can often frighten us or turn us off. So if you wish, please adjust the words you use to lend you meaning for reality.

The only reason some of us have difficulty bringing willingness forward is beliefs that may dictate something else. Many hold beliefs that are based in fear of knowledge, because knowledge is within and beliefs are focused outside. Why do beliefs often despise knowledge? The answer is simple, if we are truthful with ourselves. It's because with knowledge, our beliefs may become falsified, and we must put them behind us. We learned earlier that beliefs cannot give knowledge a lesson.

Believing has no place for true inner peace, only because a belief is too busy analyzing its doubts and raising more conflict as it worries over fear. In the background of your mind there is always the little voice asking questions: "What if?" or "Has it ever been proven?" or "I'll believe it when I see it."

Think about it. Were many of us not taught since childhood to believe in God—yet we fear Him? The fear of anything is always the fear of losing something. We may fear losing paradise, or Heaven, for example—which also implies a belief in the opposite, the "hellfire" concept we dreamed up somewhere along the line. We believe this to be a frightening fact. But what does true knowledge tell you? Does the power of the real Universe truly need a hell?

Allowing Knowledge to Find You

The writings of Henry David Thoreau have found their way to me. They inspire me with what I need and open my mind so that knowledge comes forward. Thoreau questioned the beliefs passed along by his forebears. In his famous book, *Walden*, he wrote: "If a man does not keep pace with his companions perhaps it is because he hears a different drummer." Thoreau challenges us by adding, "Let him step to the music he hears, however measured or far away."

Don't get me wrong. I do understand that our beliefs are intended to give structure and purpose to our lives in a world quick to destroy that same structure. But we must be careful in remembering that when we do believe in something, we will try to make it true for ourselves. Rather, we must understand our well-intended beliefs as right-minded perceptions, which are inspirations for welcoming positive change and alterations in patterns. Then we can use real vision to see beliefs for their intended use, which is to leave space for the power of knowledge to enter.

Let's face it, when we're left with doubt, conflict seems to find its way into the intended direction we're heading. Therefore, rather than believe in what God wants for you, leave it open as a simple perception and allow knowledge to find you in time. How much time? This is up to the Holy Spirit in His task of bringing it to you, as it reflects the purpose of the whole. Instead of your ego drawing to wholeness like a leech, only to make separate wholes, the wholeness of the Universe will come to you. Why? Because wholeness needs you; otherwise, it lacks, which I assure you is impossible. Wholeness will come to you by the knowledge brought forward in you as being one with It.

Since the ego is afraid to be in conflict with God, it will work diligently at drawing you further into believing you are separate from God. It will try to make your split, fragmented, confused, and worrisome thoughts conflict. These are the fearful, conflicting thoughts that bring on an attack. But because the mind cannot attack, the ego will persuade you to believe in yourself as a body. The ego-based mind, not having knowledge of God, cannot see you as you truly are. It does, however, see you through a mirror of guilt. It becomes aware of this weakness and wishes you to be on its side, but not as your real self. The ego cannot face you in Truth.

The real and secure you knows that when you are through using your body for its intended purpose, you'll peacefully lay it aside. The fearless you will move on within eternity, just as joyful as you've always been. The ego resists your moving on and is always trying to bring your mind to its promising, but never peaceful, thought system. It never wants to be a part of or joined with Truth; thus it promotes belief making. The ego will cry out as it chants: "You gotta believe!"

The ego-based mind tries to make beliefs and hang onto them, so your vision to the light of knowledge is obscured. These are the beliefs that try to make you afraid of new and alternative ways of considering not only life, but yourself and the Divine.

For example, isn't much of humankind in constant conflict over right and wrong beliefs in just about everything? One group may say, "Our way is the only way to believe" or "This religion is the very first rock the church was built on" or "This holy text is the only true word of God." These and many other beliefs keep our minds dividing and fragmenting its allegiance to separate kingdoms, but the actual commitment is only to confusion, doubt, and let's not forget fear.

Does it really matter which version of any religious scripture gives some more comfort and understanding than it may for someone else? The Holy Spirit's interpretation of anything is the same as your true vision, rather than what someone may suggest is best for you. Therefore, it really only matters to you and the path of your true free will.

Any belief you accept, apart from what you truly know, is obstructing God's voice in you. There is no other body, or organized group of bodies, be it religious, political, or otherwise, that knows you as who you truly are. This true essence of yourself is your holiness, which is your Divinity and is whole.

If you choose not to accept this knowledge of yourself, then you are not accepting the power of the Universe as it is intended for you. By not accepting this power as yours, you are then seeing God's creation as weak, and the weak are those who are angry and attack. This weakness is exactly what the dream of separation, or ego, is all about.

Chapter 30
Denial as a Defense

My good friend in mind, Henry David Thoreau, wrote these famous words in his book, *Walden*: "There are a thousand hacking at the branches of evil to one who is striking at the root."

He went on to write about how every day we accuse, attack, and blame others for our own failures, because it seems they don't necessarily see things our way. Often we look at these others as being in denial of reality, when all along the focus and attention on ourselves has been on the unreal. This is the illusion of who and what we think we are.

I'd like to share with you a brief parable, told to me when I was in my early thirties by an older gentleman and close friend who is no longer with us physically. Lyman was his name, and he still lives on while breathing eternal air. My memory of him is vast and grateful.

Lyman always portrayed himself as taking the bumps and grinds of life lightly and with peace. I can still hear his wit with a clear picture of the two of us fishing from the edge of the huge pond on the wooded acreage at his home. He wanted me to understand that "Releasing ourselves is the first step toward realizing our own power." He made us both laugh about my trying to grasp the notion that nothing is beyond our control. His message was that "We're only victims to ourselves." At a time when I was struggling over personal problems, he injected a bit of humor into my dilemma while sharing this story with me, that at the time helped me to sort things out. He had a title for this parable, but my memory has not retained it over the years. I've since given it my own title: "Don't Struggle to Find Knowledge."

There once was a great teacher who had many disciples dedicated to learning truth and inner knowledge. One day one of his students came to him and said, "Master, all I want is to be as peaceful as you. Please give me the secret to your knowledge." The teacher stood up and quietly walked away.

A week later that same student came to him again and said, "Master, I know you have the secret. All I want is to be intuitive like you. Please do not hold the secret from me." Again, the teacher turned his back on the student. After another week the student again persisted. "Master, I know you have the secret I so desperately seek. I will not rest until you give it to me."

This time the teacher asked the student to follow him down a path to the river. The teacher took off his clothes and jumped into the water. He told the student to do the same. The young man jumped in, but before he was able to get his feet beneath himself, the teacher grabbed him in a choke hold and held him underwater. The student struggled and fought, but the teacher was too strong for him. Finally, the teacher let go and the student rushed to the surface, gasping for air.

After a moment the teacher said, "When you were beneath the water, what was the one thing on your mind?" The student wiped the water from his eyes and answered, "Getting a breath of air. All I could think about was wanting air."

The teacher looked deep into the student's eyes and said, "When you want more inner knowing and peace the same way you wanted air, I will not have to teach you anything. Your enlightenment will teach me."

Our Focus on the Unreal

That little story keeps me from searching for my destiny and being afraid I'll never find it, because if I see what's in my heart as being real and accessible as the air I breathe, then my true free will is reflected into this world. Individuals everywhere live in constant fear of being defeated or failing before they ever set out to accomplish their dreams, because of their attention and focus on the unreal. As our awakening occurs, that fear will have to be released. If it's not, then the world will not awaken peacefully, but the Holy Spirit will not allow this. It's impossible to reawaken at Home in Heaven while in pain and anger and frustration. These kinds of things don't exist.

Peace will inevitably awaken to peace, because that is all that exists behind the dream of separation. The goal is to arrive at this event with as much ease as possible, in peace and joy. Releasing such fear is achieved by teaching and learning through the Christ-Mind, in Truth.

You may have been wondering, what really is the difference between the Little Garden Society and the Christ-Mind? There really is no difference. The Little Garden Society is simply a form of logical inference, an analogy, if you will, that brought you to the Christ in yourself. If I had written too soon about all the individuals seeing themselves as Christ, I may have lost the attention of some readers and not achieved the train of thought I hope I have offered. Remember, it's the meaning we are after, not the words. The point of the Society is to give your mind a sense of helpful and sharing unity, which you are a part of and is what the Christ-Mind provides.

The sharing of mind I'm talking about was an instinct in the people I've mentioned throughout this book, whether they realized it or not. The point is that I was assisted when I needed the help, so my purpose would advance to the next stage. The spirit of life in everyone has a way of helping us heal, even in a time when the physical presence of someone has left us. Are these people then idols? Hardly. We certainly cannot view Christ as an idol when He is who each one of us truly is. Could we ever call eternal wholeness an idol?

Joy is the way to healing and releasing fear. Whenever you keep from sharing the joy in yourself with others, don't you feel deprived? We all do. There are times when we want to share our joy by shouting it everywhere. It's impossible to deny part of our joy, just as we cannot love in part. No one can experience part of his or her love or joy that is felt during elation, and save the other part for later, when we might experience misery.

It is simply impossible to deny joy or love. Trying to deny something holds no power, but you can give it power from your mind, which is limitless. If you use the power of your mind to deny the reality of who you are, then your reality will be gone for you. Then the true reality of who you are cannot be appreciated.

This is the answer to why you don't know who you are and your purpose here. This is how you miss the idea of the Sonship as being yourself. You may have doubts and questions, just as I still often have, and the voice in your head might say, "I have these great ideas and I really want to express them to the world." You move forward in feeling you can help others, but then you ask yourself a question from doubt, like "Who am I, anyway, to even consider such a notion?"

Have you ever felt this way before, even slightly? Have you ever had ideas that excited you to no end, only to keep them hidden for whatever excuse, and then regretted your decision later? Well, I surely have.

In writing my book, my editor friend, Carol, whom I briefly introduced earlier, has convinced me in her own unique style to not be afraid to bring forward in my mind what it is I truly want to say. She has convinced me to let go of any spin or sidetracking of an issue. Likewise, at about the same time as Carol's lesson sank in, I discovered a lesson in the student workbook of *A Course in Miracles*, that I should not try to interpret the *Course*'s principles as others do. Then later, in the *Manual for Teachers*, I was specifically instructed to use my own unique interpretation when extending my thoughts of the *Course*'s content.

The lesson in all this, for myself and for you, is that all along, deep within, I already knew this. But for some strange reason I would use spin or sidetracking, and concern myself with learning the interpretations of other well-known teachers of *A Course in Miracles*. Why? Because I was afraid of showing all of me to the world. I was afraid of being judged to whatever degree the world might judge me. I thought I needed to preserve some of me for another time.

So now, with this out of the way and all the cards on the table, let's move forward. Let's see how we can heal doubt and gain confidence by clearly being ourselves. You are the only reality that exists, and you cannot appreciate yourself only in part.

Nurturing Healing

You are the Sonship, and this is why you cannot love or appreciate only in part. When you appreciate yourself, what purpose does this serve? It feeds growth and nurtures healing.

You either do or do not appreciate yourself. You are either using Christ or illusion, the Holy Spirit or ego, as your thought system. There is no middle ground. This is why if we deny any part of our own true reality, we have lost the awareness of all of it. Often we use denial as a defense, which makes it capable of being used positively, or it can be decidedly used negatively. When denial is used in a negative fashion it is destructive, because it will be used for attack.

In this way we may accuse a person of being in denial because his or her views don't see eye to eye with ours. Or the group we belong to may judge a person as an outcast, declaring that the person lacks belief. Does this sound familiar?

But let's be real here and take this to a positive level. If we are alert to the Holy Spirit as an aspect of who we are, denial as a defense can help us positively to recognize a part of reality, a part of who we are, and deny anything else as an illusion. Please bear with me here.

Yes, you can accept the accusation that you are in denial. It is a fact that you do, indeed, deny illusion and choose only to accept what you are as knowledge, but not by believing. You can carry out this denial, simply and understandably, because you "know" better. Once again, as we said earlier, this may seem like an arrogant stance. But it is received this way only by an ego-based mind. The wrong-mindedness in you may feel guilty by seeing it as arrogant, but the right-mindedness in you knows the truth. A gut feeling?

We can feel positive about our gut feelings, accepting them as intuition and the power of our own reality. By not denying our intuition, or not putting it off as a whim or lucky guess, we can learn to appreciate its power as entirely the reality of who we are. Intuition is your own thought and is who you are.

An intuition is something we know, unlike our beliefs. The mind is too powerful to exclude the reality of real thoughts, or we can call these Divine Thoughts. Let's move on so we can come to know the real, magnificent you.

Chapter 31
Giving Intuition a Chance

When an individual acts against you with any type of attackful thoughts or gestures, he or she is offering you the opportunity to bless him or her. What does giving a blessing entail?

First of all, it surely does not mean getting all caught up with the idea of special outside powers that you may call in by using rituals or forms of prayer. Blessing does not entail waving your hand over an individual's head, followed by religious or mystical words, or sprinkling droplets of special water onto a group in order to bless a crowd. These types of things do not bestow blessings in themselves, *unless* you are using real vision to look beyond the symbolism and feel truth in that. Remember, it's the meaning you convey that is important, rather than indicating a magic formula can heal anyone or help them to feel better.

A true blessing does involve forgiveness, whereby you are overlooking ego-based behavior. Once you overlook the ego you can look beyond it, and then see your brother/sister for who they truly are. This is a blessing because it is truthful.

A blessing may also mean extending the joy of yourself, while at the same time understanding within yourself that the other person's anger and negativity are not real, and are simply errors made by wrong-minded thinking. A blessing can also mean remaining calm while another person vents to you. It may be in your knowing when to speak and when not to speak.

Whatever you can do to get him or her to see even a glimpse of their loving self is a successful attempt at blessing a brother/sister. Let's not get all hung up on the religious meaning of a particular word, such as "blessing," but do let's concern ourselves with the true meaning, that of extending a sense of love and caring for others. This is what heals and promotes true forgiveness.

Actually Being What You Want to Be

As mentioned earlier in this book, if someone is attempting to cause you physical harm it is advisable you do something safe, such as remove yourself physically if help is not available. But this is not the type of attack I want to discuss here. I'm speaking of what it is you are denying in another person by not overlooking, and then looking beyond, ego-based behavior or attitudes, which is what you think is lacking in yourself. You must consider what lies beyond it all. Your own wrong-mindedness needs to be forgiven first. You are looking beyond your own ego-based thoughts, aren't you? If you are, congratulations, because it is so necessary in having what you want. What you have, so will you be.

Every response you make is determined by what you think you are, and this *thing* that you want to be, and which you already are, will determine every response you make. For instance, if I want to be an example of success by living in peace, my way of dealing with life will be through peaceful measures. Peace will be the outcome.

By now you should understand that to be what you *want* to be does not require any special blessing from God, because you already have it forever. Often we will hear or talk about a successful person as being "special" and "blessed" by God. What these individuals have is their own blessing—their own ability to acknowledge their true free will. It's not wished for. They have it and express it outwardly. It is an abundance they reflect from what they are within.

The ego, which you made from your separated thoughts, may cause you to picture yourself as deprived, unloved, vulnerable, and alone. How can any of this make you feel real about who you are? But you can easily escape such self-images by letting go of them, and not looking back. This is easy to do once you appreciate the fact that this picture of yourself is not what you are about. You just need to express yourself differently.

Next, don't perceive this lack in anyone else, or you will be accepting it as you see yourself to be. As long as there is such a word as "perception," your brother/sister is the mirror in which you see the image of the guilt in yourself. The doubt and fear follow.

We made perception when we first perceived guilt in our choice to separate our identity from our Source. We continue to pass along these perceived notions as if they were knowledge, from generation to generation. Perception, whether based on guilt or otherwise, is not created, but is made, and therefore it will remain with us only until the Sonship becomes completely whole. We become whole by accepting ourselves, each of us, as the Christ-Mind.

If you can understand this, then perception of anything will remain as your stepping stone to knowledge—a tool, so to speak, if it is used right-mindedly. This will allow yourself to naturally sense your own realness, which is the process of bringing wholeness to you. Think of darkness when it is exposed to light. The dark becomes the light. As wholeness arrives, the ego-based mind will fade. All that will remain is true knowledge.

For the remainder of time in this world, however, not all of our right-minded perceptions will shift to knowledge. This is okay, because our true intent is of the right-mind, and this leaves our thought process of total right-mindedness in control over illusion.

What Do You Value?

Positive perceptions are not all lasting ones, but even these do support your direction. The positive perceptions that don't last are not illusory, but only an error. Your intent is what holds value.

Illusions, however, are investments made by the ego with full intentions of being separate. They will stick with you as long as you value them. Values are powerful mental judgments. The ego likes its own judgments. The way to cancel illusions from your mind is to withdraw all value from them, and the illusion will have no life for you. They will be gone from your mind.

Ask yourself this: What is it I am valuing within my mind that doesn't feel right for me? And, what am I not valuing that feels like intuition? Think about this seriously and often. What does your intuition tell you? I am not referring to wannabe-type thoughts. I mean real, gut-wrenching, positive, for certain, intuition.

The gift of life and your success is yours to give, because it is your joy and was given to you. Don't confuse this with your body, the *dream* of life. All form is an illusion. Your life is beyond illusion, from before you projected a thought as an image you then identified as yourself. What rests peacefully beyond this image perceived as a body is the real, loving, and magnificent you.

Don't hide it, or you will be unaware of this gift only because you haven't been giving it, or better yet, extending it. In this you are depriving others. You can't make something unreal come alive. Therefore, you must begin extending this gift that you are, the "jewel" in you, so that the knowledge of yourself may easily come forward in your mind. When this happens, the whole Sonship will greet you and offer you what you need. This is pretty much what happened when I stumbled into *A Course in Miracles*, and how it opened up my mind.

A Step through the Threshold

All confusion you incur comes from not extending life, because you're not operating by your true free will. No one can do anything real, including being joyful, when they operate as if separate from their Source. Can the light switch on the wall in your kitchen operate successfully if disconnected from the wiring? A dark cooking area could result in your adding the wrong ingredient to the meal you're preparing. Then you'd have to eat in the dark, improperly nourished, on bad food—a not-so-good experience.

If you can only, and simply, live His Way, you will know who you are. Then, teaching His Way will keep you from forgetting who you are. I say "teaching" because everything we do is a lesson in some manner. Be sure to understand this in all whom you encounter daily. Then consider yourself among them in mind, not of body. This helps you to become more aware of wholeness.

What if each one of us on this planet of seven billion individuals were to live by intuition? This would be great! But would each of us always be intuitively correct all the time? Of course not. This is also great. Why? Because His Way will keep us on the path of right-mindedness all the time. This is where our thoughts and perceptions will begin stepping through the threshold to knowledge, and more important, Truth would be the foundation. Believing in "this" or "that" would be gone from our minds, and we would be perceiving a pathway for Truth. The arrival of full Atonement would occur much, much sooner.

By using intuition, we may experience world peace. All of our actions from the Truth will be the way we lead our lives, and the Holy Spirit will be happy to guide each individual to the right place at the right time, just as He does now. But in this sense we would be much more responsive, with far less pain in the undoing of errors—correction made easier, with far less serious, lengthy healing needed.

Give your brothers/sisters the appreciation God accords them always, because they are the Son of God, whole with you, and one with Him. You cannot be apart from them because you're not separate from God. Therefore, the intuition of the whole Son, the Sonship, is also that of God. Since God does not need intuition, it is His Word that identifies your direction in life. His Word has no letters of the alphabet with space between them. His Word is your knowledge.

So relax to your intuitive thoughts about the Divine, and love it as who you are. You may not always be correct, but you will be right-minded in your intent. This is God's gift to you as yourself. You will never know your own perfection until you give your intuition a chance. Consider it a step through the threshold of Heaven.

Chapter 32
An Exercise: Offer It and Ask for It

Once I am released from prison there will certainly be quality time needed to not only unwind, but to unravel myself as well, both physically and mentally. The stress due to severe anxiety is intense and takes a serious toll on the body. I can feel my muscles knotted and kinked and twisted up like a rope—the kind you would see on a dock, tightly binding a boat.

I can foresee a treatment program with a caring massage therapist who can professionally knead, iron out, and limber up this taut rope—not to mention another type of professional therapist whom I can talk with, and who will help me with mental knots. It's my own right-mindedness that tells me this will be helpful as well. This is also why, while in prison, I take myself often to that quiet area in my mind and simply listen for guidance.

A Course in Miracles teaches us, "the one Teacher is in all minds and He teaches the same lesson to all." The Holy Spirit always teaches us of the unlimited sharing capabilities that are infinite in each of us. As a Son of God, we have an inestimable worth. Those who attack do not know how they are blessed. We must give and receive of the abundance we each have. We each have areas of strength another individual can use. So let's not dwell on illusions of scarcity, or we will perceive ourselves as lacking.

Being that the ego-based mind is an illusion, it doesn't believe that it is responsible for itself, and being out of accord with God it clearly does not trust anyone or anything. The ego doesn't realize Truth as all there is to real life.

In this exercise we seek to go beyond the illusion of our dreaming, ego-based mind and go directly to our Source. I will share a meditation I have found successful as a way to communicate with everyone as a whole. Yes, we will connect directly with the Sonship, which is directly in union with God, our Source of life. We will get to that place beyond our own projections that keep us separate from the whole Son of God—the illusory projections that cause us to think we are lacking.

Each one of us is the Will of God. Our true free will involves expressing this as so. Do not accept anything else or you'll be denying what you are. By denying this you'll believe that attack is inevitable in order that you, as well as others, may attain their free will. The result then is never achieving, thus delaying the Atonement. This is where we get the idea of a "dog-eat-dog world" or "Life's a bitch, then we die."

This kind of thinking is why you must learn to communicate beyond the ego, or body—in other words, going over (beyond) its illusory superiority. You are inferior to nothing in your realness. Try to see the Love of God as never-ending resources, abundant for your needs in living a life of purpose and true freedom.

This abundance is natural and is created by us all as a whole, and is ready to be received by us individually, simply by our asking for what we need. There are no requirements, such as sacrificing in one area in order to receive in another. Your brothers/sisters are a part of you, just as you are a part of God. The peace and joy you are capable of is rooted in understanding this. You will begin to see creation as wholly real, wholly perfect, and wholly desirable when you put your scarcity thoughts behind you.

In the remainder of this book I'll write about firsthand examples of creation through miracles that exemplify the wholeness of the Sonship in action. You will learn that you lack nothing; however, you may simply not be drawing from this abundance in the area in which you think you lack. You may have been blind to the fact that the Sonship has an infinite supply waiting for you. The Sonship wants you to have it. Whatever you believe is missing is ready and willing to be given to you. But you must be ready and willing to receive this offering.

Receiving What You Ask For

Before you begin this exercise session, think of the areas where you feel some scarcity, or some incompleteness or incompetence, or something you're having difficulty with that leaves you feeling uncomfortable, stressed, or insecure.

For example, often there are times I find it difficult to reach that state of calm or quietness of mind. It's necessary for me so I can get in touch with my own creativity. The ego chatter going on in my mind, and then sent to my brain, seems to wind me up as tightly as a rope, disturbing my quiet and calm state. Try to narrow it down for yourself. What is your weak area and what is your free will?

Next, think of an area or areas about which you feel pretty good or secure, a certain positivity or confidence level, or even professionalism. For me lately, it has been an unusual surge of inner strength and motivation that leads me to my writing goals, even while in prison. This keeps me inspired, and now that I have Carol, the editor, and her kind guidance, I've learned much about my own writing ability in little time—*and greatly improved. (*Editor's note!) I feel surges of inspiration that I know are infinite.

At times, however, I feel short on the calm and quietness of mind I need, and prison can certainly do this. I'm not looking for excuses or placing blame. This calm is important to me because it supports my strength. Keep in mind that these areas often change, and when they do we simply bring to our minds, once again, areas of the abundance to draw from.

The successful meditation I use here entails alerting the Sonship to this strength I have to offer, in its infinite supply, so that others in need may draw from it. Of course my own supply of this inner strength may differ from the degree others have to offer. Likewise, the forms of strength or peace or joy or other inner qualities differ in all of us. This is why the Holy Spirit sorts it out and matches it up. Also, remember that in no way will it decrease my own supply when I give it.

On the other hand, I will receive from the Sonship the exact and specific form of calm and quietness I ask for. If you are chuckling over this in disbelief, just accept it as an ego antic, and if you're serious about learning this, please stay with me. The ego will tire and fade out of the picture in due time. The point is to stay above and beyond the ego here. If you cannot, and ego interference is too extreme, don't worry. Just try again later, as I've often had to do in my beginning stages of practicing this exercise. You have not failed as long as your intent is there and you are truly honest. If so, that in itself is pure knowledge. Time will set the ego aside—a tool used by the Holy Spirit.

Now let's begin. Use your own favorite meditation technique; my own is to focus on the rhythm of my breathing. Length of time in this meditation does not matter, but achieving a relaxed state of your body does. Put yourself at ease. I turn my attention to an in-and-out rhythmical sensation of breath. Next, I speak the following words in my mind with each inward and outward breath:

I now offer the Sonship my inner strength,
which is successfully now sustaining me.
I have had some incredible endurance lately,
and I offer this too.

As I continue to focus on the breath, I add:

I appreciate while accepting your offerings
of calm and quietness of mind.

I repeat both statements in a sequence that feels comfortable for me, and for an amount of time that I feel is adequate. However, don't limit yourself to giving and receiving as you practice this.

In my case, for example, there may be times when I am content and all I am doing is giving my inner strength, or whatever else I feel abundant in. Before each writing session I always take about thirty seconds or so and let the Sonship know I give all that I am in my thoughts to that particular session. A writing session for me could consist of only a few minutes, but in most cases is a few hours of nonstop thought and writing. When I have completed a session I feel as though I have been in touch with myself at my deepest level. I feel good, in the same way as giving a friend a gift.

On the other hand, there have been times when I'm only asking for what I need, and not offering. Remember, there are no rules for reciprocation whatsoever. The infinite abundance we all share is owned by everyone.

There have been times when ego interference gives me a lack of confidence in my writing goals, and in anything else, for that matter. It's a fog I can't seem to penetrate, though I do realize it's only temporary, since the realization of my ego has become an ongoing part of my awareness. Therefore, it has become easier for me to sit through the fog as it gradually lifts. At such times, here is what I ask:

I will that there be light shed
on helping me to create the right message
for others to grasp and appreciate.

It never fails for me. The fog always lifts in due time.

Be sure to use your own chosen words, based on what you feel you need, and/or what you'd like to give. But be certain to remember that no matter how often you ask, it will not affect the infinite abundance available to you at all times.

So relax and enjoy this by finding a style that suits you. Results are usually immediate. You will find that you will not only "have" what you give and ask for, but you will also "be" it, as in "all you can be." These gifts are Heavenly, which is what you are. This exercise works, so develop it, use it, and become of the abundance.

PART V
MIRACLES

Chapter 33
The Wine Country

During my thirties I spent much time in the Clearwater, Florida, area, not only expanding my business practice as a financial advisor, but also playing some good golf. The golf course proved to be a great place to meet with other business professionals in their own spare time and to take advantage of the Florida sunshine.

One lovely sunny afternoon at Lansbrook Golf Course in Palm Harbor, while grinding away at my own swing on the driving range, I met Jon Phillips. I could see that this nice man, about my same age, had undoubtedly been at the game of golf for many years. No golfer could have developed a swing like his without years of devotion to the craft. I watched in amazement as he used his small, slender frame to pound ball after ball off the practice tee, just as precisely as possible. It couldn't have looked any finer. Even an inexperienced golfer, someone who had never touched a golf club before, would be able to spot a talent as Jon played.

I soon learned that Jon had built a small communications company that handsomely funded his golfing addiction, as well as supporting a lovely family and personal life. The two of us were soon off to a good start at par in a great friendship.

After a couple of rounds of golf together, Jon invited me to become a regular in his Monday and Thursday golf league that played at other courses in addition to Lansbrook, which I was calling my home golf course. I accepted, and discovered by talking with others in that group of great guys that Jon was considered by many to be one of the best golfers not only in the area, but in the entire state of Florida.

Jon had won all of the local tournaments "hands down," over and over, and several trophies from state and regional events as well, never having declared himself to professional status. Some affluent area business owners formed a group to offer Jon financial backing, urging him to head to the pro circuit. They wanted to help him pursue the PGA Tour. These guys—

mostly older men, some retired—could see themselves in Jon. There was nothing in it financially for them. They just wanted to see a local talent prove himself in the bigtime golf world, a chance they wished they'd had themselves in their younger golfing days.

This would be a dream come true for almost all serious and exceptional golfers at Jon's level of play, but the offer was only for Jon and not for anyone else. If you'd ever met Jon, you would see why this good-hearted group of men wanted to help him. Jon's humble nature and personality had "champion" projected within a halo over his head. But Jon would not accept their grand sponsorship and he let go of the idea. All he would say was that it was "not what he wanted."

I would often notice others trying to make Jon feel guilty, and they would talk behind his back about not understanding why he would not take advantage of this offer—"the chance of a lifetime" as they saw it. The same individuals who criticized Jon for this would try to project an image of him as lacking belief in himself. But I could see, simply from playing competitive golf with this good guy, that this was not the case. I'd seen his composure when lining up an eight-foot, sliding, left-to-right, downhill putt, needed to win a golf match. I'd witnessed his confidence when, two strokes down with three holes to play, he needed an "up and downer" from a deep greenside bunker just to stay in contention. This man was a "player." He was always the finest of gentlemen when conceding a match, too. Jon Phillips had what many golfers could only dream of having.

Sharing

Jon and I continued to play a lot of good golf together, even away from the Monday and Thursday golf league. The more we hung out together on great golf courses all over the Tampa Bay area, the better friends we became. I found our time together rewarding. We could confide in each other and would often do so about much more than our good, bad, and ugly golf rounds.

We shared feelings about our children, wives, ex-wives, businesses, the economy and its markets, religion, racial matters, and even the possibility of world peace, which would lead us into a lengthy discussion on politics. You name it, we hashed it out. Between the two of us we figured out a way to solve world hunger, as well as a solution for the homeless population.

I once asked Jon to please expand on his answer, confidentially, as to why he would not at least give professional golf a shot. I asked if the rumors were true that he didn't believe he could actually "step it up" with the players on the big PGA Tour.

Jon knew he could trust me. He smiled with a slight chuckle and told me that he "for sure did believe he could survive" on the pro tour. But he also said that he simply "did not want it badly enough." When I asked him why he didn't want it, he told me softly, "Jim, you must understand, for me, I do believe that once I did 'step it up' to that level of play, I could make a good living on the tour."

On seeing my confused but interested expression, he then explained what I truly wanted to hear. "You see, Jim," he said. "For me to make it happen I would have to give golf my absolute best commitment and devotion. I would have to make it become my life, and I know in my heart that I'm not willing to do that." Then he added, "If I'm not *willing* to do what it takes, then I'll never be *ready* to sink those important putts."

I interrupted and asked if he could "just have fun" at it and not concern himself with the work involved. He stopped me and asked me to let him finish. "In other words, Jim, I know what it would take away from me. There would be a price involved—a sacrifice of certain personal things I don't care to mention, and this I know is not the path I truly *want* to travel on."

It seemed to me he was wasting a God-given talent, but it was surely not for me to judge. Regardless, I can say that the honesty Jon showed me was inspiring, and his unnecessary explanation was more than enough to satisfy any further curiosity I might have over the matter. That conversation actually tightened our friendship.

We talked further that evening about other topics over dinner and a bottle of wine. We'd just played a round of golf a few hours earlier, in rainy and windy conditions, and the good food and comfortable setting of the old tavern was truly a treat. An older gentleman wearing a golf visor was playing the piano in the corner of the bar area. The art and elegance of fine wine was another interest we shared, as did our wives as well. But for whatever strange reason, our wives never met each other and a foursome never materialized. I did on occasion speak with Jon's wife, Becky, however.

As Jon carefully poured some more wine into my glass and then into his, he asked me if I'd ever visited the wine country in California. He called this northern territory out west "God's Country" and said very enthusiastically that his and Becky's plan was to one day "pack it up," leave Florida, and "head for them thar hills."

The Calling

As time went by Jon and I were playing golf more and more, and our friendship was allowing him to share with me some of his plans for the move out west. He said he truly "felt a calling" to live there and explained to me how he would restart his small communications company in that area. The business had something to do with tracking information for police departments, courts of law, and similar clients.

I can still hear him saying to me that he didn't have to *believe* in his true destiny if he already *knows* what it is. I always felt inspired by Jon, not only by his flawless and fluid golf swing, but as an individual who always seemed to be pointed in a positive-minded direction, and with much balance in his life.

Some years went by, things changed for both of us as they always do, and Jon and I sort of lost touch with each other. My business was becoming more demanding of my time, with my efforts split between an office in Canton, Ohio, and another in Tarpon Springs, Florida. My time spent on the golf course was at an all-time minimum.

One thing led to another, and with the economy, the stock and bond market, my own financial situation, and my marriage on the rocks, my life was filled with stress and anxiety. I was no longer having fun. It wouldn't be long before my troubles would slam me like a wrecking ball. The agony of divorce, coupled with frightening legal problems that soon would become an indictment by a grand jury on criminal charges jolted me. I was a mess and lost.

Now Here I Am Writing to You

Here in prison I cannot describe the feeling when one sees one's name on the daily incoming mail list. For me it's a sense of being in touch with freedom. Even a short note from a family member or an old friend who hasn't forgotten you lends a sense of belonging. To feel united is freedom.

Mail call becomes an exciting part of a routine day, and is why the weekends and holidays with no mail service can seem so dismal. Unless you've been in prison, you can never begin to understand the impact of a single piece of mail.

On a particular day when I needed it most, my name appeared on the mail list at the guard's desk. As I squeezed my way through the crowd of smelly armpits and bulging tattoos, the guard already had his arm stretched out with a letter in his hand for me to grab. I didn't recognize the return address, but did notice immediately it was from California.

The letter was from my long-ago, but not forgotten, Florida golf buddy Jon Phillips, and it was plain to see he was now living in the Sonoma Valley. He had finally made it to the wine country, "God's Country." His custom return address label displayed decorative grapevines surrounding his name and address.

I was emotionally lit up with elation as I quickly counted backward in my brain to realize that it must have been fifteen years since we'd last spoken or seen each other. There he was, that sweet-swinging Jon, with me for the moment behind these block walls and steel bars. I could see with excitement he had much to fill me in on. His letter was several pages inside a bulging envelope with extra postage on it. Just by knowing Jon, I knew there had to be good things he wanted to share with me. I walked back to my bunk to savor his letter. Suddenly the volume of chaotic noise around the prison house seemed to be nonexistent.

Jon's letter described how his business, the communications company, was alive, doing well, and small-scale, just as he wanted it to be. With minimal stress which he handled well, he had plenty of free time to play competitively in Northern California's over-fifty senior amateur golf circuit. He could delegate much of the headaches of his business to his office manager, a middle-aged recent widow who loved the challenge. Jon said he paid her well above average, and she was worth every penny. He said he could trust her to keep things running smoothly while he and his wife enjoyed California—and, as first-time grandparents, their new granddaughter.

Among many other things, Jon told me his company's high-tech systems had enabled him to track me down, as well as to see for himself through court records the details of the mess I'd gotten myself into—not to mention the heartache I must have caused others. He went on to say that by just knowing me, he was well aware of my sincere regret and my apologies to those who fell victim to my irresponsible actions. He also added how glad he was to see that my case was not as serious as the court had trumped it up to be. He indicated that I should relax and expect to get through this experience while I watch it leave itself behind me. "Just hang in there" were his closing words to this treasured communication between good friends.

I paused to put his letter down briefly and thought to myself how absolutely correct he was. I just cannot believe how I allowed myself to get caught up in the actions that sent me to prison, and for those directly and indirectly affected, I take this opportunity to publicly apologize once again. There are times when we take ill-fated action and we know it. So why do we do it? Only deep within us individually do we truly know the answer. Accepting this answer is the first step in forgiving ourselves. Then we can move forward in asking others for their forgiveness.

In Jon's letter he reminisced about words of inspiration and wisdom he said I once gave him as a gift and that he still treasured today. In fact, he said he recalled those words during a difficult time in his transition to California, with the hectic move and the business being reestablished in a new state with different regulations. It was something about "change being healthy and shouldn't be frightening" that struck a chord with him.

As I put his letter into my footlocker with the intention of savoring it later, in a more relaxed time of the evening ahead, it dawned on me how we each help each other in this world and often don't realize it. All along I was thinking about how Jon had always inspired me, and now here he was thanking me for the same.

But Jon was once again back on his game, inspiring me further when I truly needed it, along with an open invitation to one day play golf with him in the hills of the wine country. I licked my "golfing chops" with a smile and kept my motivation moving forward in me with a definite and certain vision of placing the totality of these dark times in prison behind me.

I don't have to believe, because I know my good friend Jon didn't find success and happiness due to his beliefs. The ego-stroking temptation to become a star pro golfer held no power over him because he was honest with himself. He is where he is today due to the knowledge he tapped into within himself, simply by following his heart, rather than what others prescribed for him. His golf game, his brotherhood, and his family life are a clear reflection of the "jewel" that is his reality.

Chapter 34
Abundance or Scarcity as Your Choice

Ask yourself a question about your own beliefs, and be sure to answer with all honesty. Keep it to yourself, but be sincere. If you can't touch your own sincerity, you'll have difficulty having what you want.

Are you placing efforts into getting ahead in life, going along with the world's desires, or are you truly sharing ideas of peace, joy, and anything that heals or inspires you, thereby automatically inspiring others—efforts in which love reveals your truthfulness?

Take some time with this. It's a simple formula for avoiding fear and moving forward with your life. Be truthful with yourself, regardless of what the ego might be tossing around in your brain. If what you do each day is of love, then you are not wasting time as you would by projecting images of the way you *wish* things could be. Rather, you must bring life to you in the way that you *want* it to be.

Let's face it. You really can't love an image. If you believe you can, then you are living an ego fantasy, by allowing your beliefs to project images of your *wishful* thinking.

A Course in Miracles states this Truth: "Every mind must project or extend, because this is how it lives, and every mind is life."

Overriding Beliefs

It might seem to you that in the last few chapters I have come down pretty hard on the idea of beliefs. If you do feel this way, or have questioned this by doubting, please try to see that this is clearly your ego placing judgment. This gives your ego-based mind permission to make a defense. But there is nothing for you to truly defend, because there is no attack.

Our projected images make these beliefs where knowledge wants to override them. Knowledge is all about *wanting*. What it needs to get, it gets by extending itself rather than projecting a wishful image of fantasy.

But when your ego is in control over you, nothing is wanted—only wished for—and knowledge is seen as scary and intimidating. Sound familiar?

You can't have attack-type thoughts if you don't project an image of defense. Likewise, if we don't extend ourselves there can be no love in the world. This is the fundamental law that operates the mind, and it keeps everything that is real in the mind of God. Anything unreal does not enter the mind as real, because in reality it doesn't exist. But its image can be seen, and will be projected by the separated mind, which is dreaming of the unreal: all that we physically see in the dream of life. Can this physical or dream form truly be loved? In other words, do you love your loved one's body, or is it him/her, the "jewel" that she/he is, that you truly love?

Is attraction love? I speak here not only of romantic attraction, but attraction to all physical things—money, property, status, territory. Our attraction to these projections has continued to change, modify, and project conflict in a battle that only struggles for more. Then, if that's not enough, we project guilt onto ourselves and those around us, who we feel are out to take something away from us so that they may have more. We seem to derive a feeling of security in having more, and insecurity in less. When we try to give by extending ourselves, the ego likes to justify it by telling us that we're only getting rid of what we can no longer use.

However, the Holy Spirit in us knows this as the law of giving what we value by sharing it in our minds, and this is how He teaches us to extend. The ego will project an image of any such sharing or giving as sacrificing or depriving itself. The ego will turn this upside down by *believing* it has done something good by depriving itself, and it expects its due reward later.

While the ego can never understand true reality, it also cannot accept that sharing the real, such as an extension of love, *creates* abundance. It only comprehends the sharing of the unreal, or fantasy, which it believes *makes* scarcity.

My friend Jon had an image of himself on the PGA Tour that seemed exciting and attractive. But the means required for him to get there and remain there was not a picture of joy for him. He would have had to give up time with his family and his dream of moving to the wine country. In other words, playing golf for competition at that level would not have been an extension of himself, regardless of his talent.

There is one thing for certain that you do indeed know, and so do I. When we share or extend our love, we don't lose it or decrease its level of abundance in us. Actually, we feel increased love. It is not a loss and still remains in us, as well as benefiting the individuals to whom we give it. This creates abundance. Thus the thoughts of abundance or scarcity are our personal responsibility.

Does my friendship with Jon leave me with scarcity thoughts or thoughts of abundance? Ask yourself: How do your friends make this decision about you? That answer, most importantly, lies in how you see yourself. Are you lacking or are you abundant?

Chapter 35
Are You Preserving Your Beliefs?

You may think that much of this book is a discussion of the ego-based mind. But what I really want to pass on to you is a lesson I've learned on how I was able to realize my own abundance. The ego kept me from this realization for much of my adult life, but now my goal is to share my abundance with others.

We must first understand the ego's use of projection before the relationship between projection and anger can be undone by the Holy Spirit. He wants us to know *what* we must let go of.

The ego will always perceive conflict, at least always in the background of a situation. However, it also wants you to know the importance of reducing conflict, because it doesn't want conflict to be so intolerable that you simply choose to give it up. The ego is aware that it cannot survive without you having some level of conflict in your life. Therefore, the ego tries to convince you that it has the capability to free you of conflict—but it doesn't want you to have the power to free yourself. The ego strives to make you feel that you need it.

For example, consider how children carry conflict around within themselves, often induced by their own parents. Poor school performance, household chores not getting done, sibling strife, or just about anything that may linger in the growing pains of our kids can be a setup for conflict.

Often the thought process enters: "I hope my parents don't find out." Or, when a parent does find out, there may come the dreaded words: "Wait till I tell your father about this." Of course, the implied threat makes for further turmoil. But while such secrets and reactions can stimulate further conflict, we could approach the situation differently. We could choose to see errors as errors; let truth be shown so it can be known, and move on. But we seem to wish to drag conflict around with us.

The ego-based mind has its own made-up, warped versions of the laws of God, which pertain to the body taking the focus away from the mind, where real purpose exists. The ego gives our minds projected images of other bodies out on a mission to take God away from us.

Let's take a look at two major errors involved in this attempt. First of all, conflict cannot be shared just because it is projected. Keeping part of it and getting rid of another part doesn't really mean anything. Remember, teaching conflict is poor teaching, as we learned earlier, and only results in poor learning. The lesson becomes confusing, and any value in it is limited by the confusion of the teacher.

The second error is the idea that you can get rid of something you don't want by giving it away. We must not forget that giving something is how we keep it. That which we extend remains with us as it is being extended. But the ego has taught us that seeing something as outside of us means that we have excluded it from within us.

This is why the ego can't understand extension and only understands separation. This is also why those who build their lives by projecting are fearful that someone or something is always waiting to tear down their image. We may like to teach "Don't judge a book by its cover," but we resort to doing so anyway. The projection that what seems good on the outside must also be good on the inside seems to creep back in.

No one can behold an illusion about someone else without beholding it in themselves. In order not to, we would have to fragment our true One-mindedness into pieces. This is impossible, but the ego dreams that this is what it is doing with its separated projected images.

Remember, a projection is not real, but it is the best the ego can do, which is to dream. The real mind can never be aware of any such projections, which is why there can be no attack in any fashion. The belief that it can is an error the ego makes by judging, and therefore believing it has a basis for its use of projecting.

The ego doesn't understand what the mind really is, and at best sees itself as the body's brain. This is why the ego doesn't understand what you really are. Yet it depends on the mind for its survival, because the ego is our belief that the body is who we are, which is why we're so afraid of what is real. Yes, we are afraid to meet our real and true Self head-on.

The Confused State

Truly think to yourself, for a moment or so, of all that frightens you. Think of all the things that make you feel insecure about your life. The fear that we try to hide in ourselves confuses us. The ego is nothing more than a confused state of our own real and true identity that dreams, and confusion does make errors.

This is why the ego's distorted thinking misapplies the Laws of God for it misuse of its illusory power. This is also why this illusory power works diligently to teach us to fear our Creator, who resides someplace "out of sight." The ego wishes that we love what we fear as being separate from who we are. All that the ego can see is limited to the body.

But we must not be afraid of the ego, which is no different from fearing our own shadow or the shadows of others. The ego relies on our being afraid of our true potential. We made the ego by believing in it. That's all. All we need to do is get rid of our beliefs altogether and keep our focus on what we perceive, regardless whether they are wrong-minded or right-minded perceptions. That will iron itself out with the Holy Spirit's task of constant undoing and reversing our errors, along with His use of time and space.

We must not project blame onto others, or we will be *preserving* our beliefs. We must let them go, so that knowledge will open the door. Our beliefs have the door blocked. Knowledge in its purest form will come to us. When we accept responsibility for the ego's existence, we will have lain aside anger, which feeds attack.

By *not* placing blame on your errors, you accept them as yours, and the Holy Spirit will see that you do not keep them. If you don't keep them, they will also be kept away from the Sonship. Errors are simply what they are, nothing more, and are made solely by the ego. Keep in mind that anything of the ego, including the ego, fades away in time. Your body, too.

So don't worry about loss, because it's only of time and certainly is not of the eternal you. The Holy Spirit will help you to understand this as time moves along, by teaching you to perceive beyond any beliefs, because Truth is beyond all belief. This is why the ego can be completely forgotten at any time—because it is such an unbelievable belief.

Chapter 36
The Carbon Copy

Here in prison, the holiday season from Thanksgiving through New Year's Day can be a time of severe struggles. The depression in the air is palpable. This is a period when receiving mail is even more valued than the regular days of the year.

On a day just after Thanksgiving, but before Christmas, I received a letter from Nakita, the woman living in Croatia whom I mentioned earlier. She had written me only one time before this, when she somehow became aware of my spiritual path as a student of *A Course in Miracles*.

It remained a mystery to this point as to how she learned of my situation, my address in prison, and my involvement in the *Course*. It was intriguing, to say the least! I found it strange that Nakita went on to tell me that much of Croatia was Catholic, and she was raised Catholic, just as I was. She mentioned how her own involvement in *A Course in Miracles* had given her new light, a new vision in how she practices her Catholic faith. "An enhancement," she said.

Nakita added that the psychological Christic teachings in the *Course* had allowed her to more clearly perceive, rather than believe, the true function and purpose in the man, Jesus, who once walked among us. Her perceptions are not the exact same picture as my own, but they follow the same truthful path.

Nakita's letter was straightforward as she shared with me her feelings of Jesus, as a man, reaching total actualization of the Christ-Mind, and being given the power by God to help the rest of humanity reach that very same state—but within ourselves as a whole. It's up to us individually as to how we perceive or sense wholeness within, as Jesus did.

Jesus is a personal symbol in the dream of separation as the manifestation of the Holy Spirit. Having been totally healed of his own split-mind, Jesus has become One with the Spirit of God, or the Holy Spirit. In this sense—my own sense, my own perceptions as I dream of time, space, and form—Jesus lives on in spirit and shares in my reflection of the Christ-Mind, and yours too. This reflection gives us Jesus as our elder brother, the oldest sibling of the whole Sonship, if you'd like to individualize this for perception's sake. Full Atonement will interlock or interconnect our minds as one whole, complete Son of God—full awakening from the dream, oneness realized just as it always has been.

For the most part, my own ideas coincided with Nakita's: as Jesus lived within this world of fear, rather He perceived love. In His lifetime His perceived notions shifted to knowledge, whereby the Holy Spirit was realized. Every action, every word, every thought He had was guided by the Holy Spirit, and not by the ego. This is where He asks us to model Him. Jesus was able to see the ego-based mind as the dream it is. A dream is nothing; it's not knowledge; it is unreal.

The Christian religion has no real laws or rules that govern our minds as to how we truly see the life that Jesus lived. He was a spiritual teacher, and there were others before and after Him as well, who were able to understand the darkness of the ego. Jesus was able to overlook the ego, and then look beyond it to the whole Son of God, and personalize the Son as Christ, just as we all forever are. This is how He has taught us the meaning of forgiveness, and it is why He leads the way in our minds to reawaken from littleness and realize the magnitude of what we truly are.

Overwhelmed

Nakita's letter was to the point, and I was surprised by her ability to communicate in English. Some misspelled words indicated her slightly broken English, and I could perceive her Croatian accent. She was insightful with her messages, but not at all pushy.

She did, however, include a small brochure or flyer that seemed to be inexpensively self-published on a copy machine. The flyer was announcing a worldwide prayer or meditation session, depending on which method was most comfortable for each individual, to be held three days before Christmas and to last only a mere ten minutes. Its purpose was to help move forward world peace in all our minds.

I was overwhelmed with curiosity and surprise, wondering who this woman could be. In the back of my mind there were thoughts of her being some kind of a "nut." But she was so nice and easygoing and down to earth that I said to myself "What the heck" and I gave her letter and flyer my sincere attention. After all, how could I judge?

I made the decision to open up my mind to her request that I somehow participate in the meditation here from prison. She also asked that I discretely and privately pass along the information to anyone else I felt would also enjoy participating. She suggested I put my name and address on the flyer and mail it to anyone I felt would appreciate the cause.

I must admit I had thoughts along the lines of "There's a sucker born every minute," but she wasn't trying to sell me anything or pull me into anything threatening, so I dismissed the thoughts. Suddenly I trusted Nakita. Her letter was too sincere for me not to. Besides, the invitation lent me a sort of excitement. Here in prison, however, I had to be careful. I was not aware of a single other prisoner I could feel safe in sharing this with. The way rumors fly and get exaggerated, a not-so-good type of label could easily get attached to me, so asking a fellow prisoner to join me was out of the question.

I began to search my mind for at least one person I could send this information to who would not think I was "off my rocker." I needed some time to think this over. In the meantime, I decided to rewrite the entire flyer neatly by hand, since word processing by a computer is unheard of for inmates in this prison system. The prison's typewriter always has a waiting line, so I ruled that out.

My willingness discovered that carbon paper could be purchased in the commissary, however. So I proceeded to rewrite the flyer on carbon paper, securing one carbon copy of my original. I now had a clear copy and an original to announce this worldwide meditation session. Here it is, in case you'd like to use it in whatever fashion you may choose:

An Invitation to Join In and Think About the Joy of Attaining World Peace

From: Jim Nussbaumer (plus my address in prison)

Dear Friend,

The Holy Spirit will be glad to take a few peaceful moments off our hands and carry them around the world, where pain and misery and suffering rule, and where peace of mind is desperately sought after or simply needed. He will not overlook one open mind that will accept the healing gifts they bring, and He will lay these peaceful thoughts everywhere. The Holy Spirit knows they will be welcome.

The goal is to increase the healing power each time someone accepts them as his or her own thoughts, and uses them to heal. Each gift of peace and healing will be multiplied a thousandfold, and tens of thousands more, and on, and on. It will then be returned to you and will surpass in might.

A society of minds invites you to join us by using the following simple words for this prayer/meditation session where the Holy Spirit speaks through everyone, so we can help in the healing needed around the world.

Peace be to me, the holy Son of God.
Peace to my brothers and sisters who are one with me.
Let all the world be blessed with peace through us.

The Little Garden Society is a society of minds everywhere with a purpose to help all minds around the world to heal through the attainment of inner peace of mind. Advertisement is not the goal, but minimal ego-based thought is. It is, however, asked that you be "true to yourself" and have a "willingness" to help heal the world from conflict of all kinds, just by your thoughts through the peace and love you are able to extend. Individuals of the Little Garden Society are scattered around the world and focus themselves wherever violence, attackful thoughts, and unsettledness prevail.

There are no strings attached, no credit cards, no money, just joy. To join us from the privacy of your own home on December 22, 2010 at 9:30 PM Eastern time, peace and love and forgiveness need only be your focus. This would mean 8:30 PM Central time, 7:30 PM Mountain time, and 6:30 PM Pacific time, and so on, around the world.

This meditation/prayer session will last for only ten (10) minutes. The purpose is to bring unity, or oneness of mind, to everyone, however-so-briefly it may occur. The length of time in which we touch each other will not matter. Regardless of time, inner peace is the resulting goal. If inner peace may be realized only for a moment, our goal will have been achieved.

After I finished rewriting this flyer with carbon paper, all sorts of negative thoughts began twirling in my mind. I actually laughed at myself for being "such an idiot." Although earlier in the day I had suddenly had an urge to trust Nakita, now I was beginning to wonder if this was some kind of game she was playing with my vulnerable side, being that I was a prisoner. Regardless, something urged me to just press forward.

One completed carbon copy was ready to go somewhere, though I was still thinking about whom to mail it to. I had already decided I would keep the original for myself. But I was still swinging back and forth in my mind as to whether I'd actually mail it at all. Even if I found someone, I was periodically haunted by doubts about the validity of the entire project, plus I was afraid of making a fool of myself. But when I actually thought about it some more, I laughed at myself again. Only this time it was more like laughing *with* myself. It hit me that I had nothing else to look forward to for the holidays anyway, so with that state of mind I decided to go forward and not look backward.

Chapter 37
Selfishness Versus Self-Fullness

Two or three days went by, and now the haunting voices in my head were calling me a "nut" louder than ever before, for falling for such a seeming prank. "That's all it could be," I would try to convince myself. Some sort of prank to tease or play around with prisoners. But I also started thinking, "Why am I being so hard on myself? After all, my intent is good."

I quickly sided with the fact that my ego was raising a fuss over the matter. But why be defensive? No attack was involved. I decided to take the pressure off myself and just have fun with the entire idea. What could it harm if true joy within myself would be the worst outcome of participating in the meditation?

Surprisingly, right at that time I received a letter from my old prison friend William, who had been released and was now enjoying his freedom with his two sons, who are both close to my age. At eighty-one years old, William was sharp as a tack. He had spent two and a half years in prison for a nonviolent offense so minor that it should never have incurred a prison sentence. The State of Ohio's tough-on-crime stance, which garners it much money from the federal government, is a "hard rock to bust." Don't get me wrong; I've lived next to many who certainly need to be in prison. The point is that it can make for tragic miscarriages of justice when a prison identification number only represents the sound of "ka-*ching*." But this is the subject matter for a future book.

Getting back to the subject at hand—William was the only other prisoner with whom I had ever shared any type of Divine Thoughts. And I had held back, even with William, on conversing about *A Course in Miracles*. I had just never seemed to have the right amount of readiness to share what I'd learned. I needed more time, I thought. Besides, *A Course in Miracles* is not intended as some sort of recruitment device. The esoteric nature of the *Course* must be respected.

After filling me in on his health, his news, and other small talk, William's letter asked a question that raised my eyebrows a bit. He went on to say that when he was in prison, he often noticed me lying on my top bunk with my face glued to a big blue book with gold lettering. Of course, William was referring to *A Course in Miracles*.

He went on to say that he'd noticed I seemed to be quite private and protective over the book and never discussed it with anyone. He also noticed the consistent hours on end I was enthusiastically writing. He added that while he was in prison, something inside him suggested he not ask me, and that if I was ever willing and ready to share it with him, then he trusted that I would. But now he was asking me to fill him in on what I had been so involved with.

I immediately began asking myself if I should write William a detailed letter explaining my devotion as a student of the *Course*. But what would I say in a letter? I did not feel comfortable having to explain myself and my knowledge, along with my experience, through the mail. It was different with my communication with Nakita because she had been a student for some time.

The Carbon Copy Mailed

One thing I did know for certain: I was going to be careful in honoring the esoteric quality of the principles contained in *A Course in Miracles*. Everyone has their own interpretation of the *Course*, though similar, with Truth as the common theme. I never wanted anyone to feel the *Course* is being pushed on them, or sold, or to feel I wanted them to convert from their religious faith. This is not what *ACIM* intends to do. Moreso, it has been proven to enhance an individual's current spiritual path, just as Nakita had written me about, saying her Catholic faith had been inspired and enriched.

Keep in mind that no church or religion affiliates itself with *A Course in Miracles*; it just so happens that Nakita is a Catholic. The *Course* is not religion, but it a psychological interpretation of Christic philosophy.

Once I gave William's question some time to soak in, I was simply guided to mail him the carbon copy of the meditation announcement, along with a note letting him know I had received it from Nakita in Croatia. But I needed to mail the letter immediately, because December 22, the night of the worldwide session, was only two weeks away. I included an explanation in the note that the flyer was describing a similar direction to the path I am on, and that I hoped to one day soon be out of prison so I could answer his question in a more satisfying way. With that said, the carbon copy was on its way to William.

Again to my surprise, he responded immediately upon receiving it, replying with a short note on a generic postcard, thanking me for the invitation. He added apologetically that this sort of thing was not for him, and that the church he had been involved with for many years had enough going on for the holidays to keep him busy and peaceful in mind.

However, with a tone of excitement, showing me positivity, William added that he didn't think I would mind that he had mailed that carbon copy to his sister, who lives out west. This was fine with me. In fact, his effort gave me a sense of relief, just knowing that I had done my part. I kept a thought alive in the back of my mind that William's sister might be enthused and become involved in this ten-minute meditation for world peace. I put the matter aside and went on with my daily routine here in prison, getting by one day at a time, studying the *Course* while continuing to write and improve my God-given craft.

I also began thinking a lot about Nakita, and her message to me about how the *Course* has her seeing a new self-fullness. I tried to picture what kind of new insight she may be receiving now by going to Catholic mass. Whatever it was interested me, because for much of my life I had found much of Catholic mass services to be boring.

Nakita had told me she was able to see Jesus as the leader of Atonement, waiting and holding her place securely in the interlocking and interwoven chain of minds. She felt that when full Atonement is finally achieved, this would be the "promised land." It's not a physical piece of soil or location at all, but is a union of minds, reawakened and at-one. We must be more concerned about the psychology of it all, rather than the strong emphasis on the body.

Nakita shared her vision of taking communion as having nothing to do with Jesus's body, as we were taught in Catholic school, but rather a symbol of being joined with the Christ-Mind, along with Jesus, who leads the way in the knowledge of this. She said this understanding, her acceptance of this, is the answer to peace everywhere.

Communion of any kind is sharing each other and is certainly peaceful. The *Course* teaches us to "Be confident that you never lost your Identity and the extensions which maintain It in wholeness and peace."

The Murder

Nakita shared with me briefly her story in the first letter and then expanded upon it with much more substance in her second letter, which included how she was led to *A Course in Miracles*. Her story is compelling. She wrote to me at length, but with no fancy exaggeration. This is why I say that her letter had substance. The forcefulness of her message left much room for descriptiveness, which I could read between her lines.

I could sense her trying to translate from Croatian to English, and she wrote well-rounded portrayals of the scenes. It was as though I could hear her accent in the words and in the spaces between them. She began a story about an occurrence in her past. While I read her words about a pounding that came at the front door of the home she shared with her husband, Armand, which woke them abruptly in the wee hours one morning, I wondered why she was telling me all this. Surely it was extremely personal.

As Nakita approached to open the door, wearing only a housecoat and slippers, a team of masked men burst into their home with guns in hand. Nakita was pushed forcefully to the floor at gunpoint. She cried out to please not shoot. She realized she and Armand were being robbed. "Don't kill me," she frantically screamed. With a gun aimed at her head she looked to her right and saw Armand charging into the room, waving a revolver. She heard a man shout, "Put the gun down! Put the gun down! Damn it, put the (frigging) gun down!" Her husband was killed instantly.

Armand and Nakita had beautiful farmland in the mountainous region between the cities of Split and Rijeka. They owned over two hundred acres of breathtaking hills and dales. It was such prime land, the government had even offered to buy portions of it from them several times, to use for a future highway system. Armand had been a collector of rare coins, many of them gold, which were stolen when the masked men ransacked their home.

The murderous men seemed to be Serbian. The Serbs and Croats were longtime enemies. A group of Serbs was known to be moving through the area, outcasts from their own country. There had been conflict in the region, the former Yugoslavia, for some years.

Nakita said that when Serbs live in any area, or even just spend time there, they think it's their own country and have total disregard for the laws of the land. They will kill, steal, and just plain do as they wish. She was convinced the masked robbers and murderers were some of the rumored Serbian outcasts. She mentioned the recent war among the Bosnians, Croats, and Serbs, which had left the area still unsettled, with hostility in the air. The details of the war are not my subject here. I'm sure the Internet can satisfy any curiosity or desire for further background you may have.

Don't Deprive Yourself

Nakita was greeted with *A Course in Miracles* shortly after Armand's murder. Everyone involved with the *Course* has their own unique story, though not all as dramatic as hers. It seems an American man, a notable guitar player who was touring and performing in the area, stayed there for a while with mutual friends. This folk singer had a copy of *ACIM* with him, and when informed of Nakita's tragic loss, he offered to review it with her over the next week.

Nakita said that once she began reading the text, she found its extremely deep content difficult to grasp, like a "foreign language," she commented. Regardless of her lack of comprehension of this abstract material, however, she did feel something stirring within her. She said it was an urging to continue that struck a chord as she absorbed its words. She knew she had to get her own personal copy of this publication, and of course she did.

Her sadness, depression, and despair over the loss of Armand began to fade as she realized that he had not totally left her at all. Of course, she terribly missed his physical presence and the life they shared together. But Nakita mentioned that it was easier for her to now understand how and why the presence he had in her life to begin with was simply part of his destiny, as well as her own.

With this understanding she also became aware that there is so much we don't understand of the "why" we must at times experience things that seem like a loss. But she also knows in her own heart to give her positive-mindedness or attitude a chance to continue her journey. Nakita knows her free will is now working wonders with the beautiful land she still lives on. All I could gather from her letters at this point was that she is using her land for the purpose of bringing joy to others.

We ourselves, just like Nakita, can only limit our creative power with ego interference. But God's Will is for us to allow peace to wave itself over interferences, and then we will realize the power of His Will, which is our free will, to be unlimited. God doesn't deprive Himself, nor does He want us to deprive or sacrifice ourselves of the gifts we have within us, even while we dream of separation. Who truly wants to have a bad dream?

Many of us remain confused over selfishness versus self-fullness. Selfishness, of course, is all about the ego and its limiting beliefs. But self-fullness is all about our unlimited perceptions of the spirit of God, which we are. These perceptions in time lead to knowledge of our unlimited abundance, whereas beliefs eventually die.

Chapter 38
Wondering if it's Real

All day on December 22, on the evening of the supposed worldwide meditation for inner peace, my ego was still haunting me through the cracks in my split-mind. Numerous questions were coming and going within me, especially as to how many people might actually be participating. Would it be only me? Was this in reality some sort of a prank? Or would it only be Nakita and myself as the lone meditators? In those moments I felt deeply uncertain.

I must say, however, that being under constant oppression and surveillance by authority as a prisoner is an understandable condition to create uncertainty. Prison is a breeding ground for unsettled thoughts of paranoia and worry; one can see it in the anxious way inmates carry themselves at times. One often wonders what will come at them next, never knowing what to expect.

I remembered in my practice as a financial advisor how I would often join in telephone conferences with many other advisors around the world. While there may have been a hundred or so participating, only some would talk while others just listened. But all participants had to check in through a central operator upon joining the call. Of course this type of arrangement for the coming night's worldwide meditation/prayer for peace was not the case. I would never know who, how many, or if any at all ever participated.

As my ego found more and more gaps to slip into in my concrete thinking, its messages grew rampant. After all, a letter had shown up for me here in prison from an unknown woman who had tragically lost her husband, and I was supposed to become overjoyed about a worldwide peace effort she'd informed me of? Was I losing my senses due to being locked up for a few years now? I'd heard it creeps up on prisoners slowly.

Or was it her? Was Nakita mentally unbalanced and had simply searched me out for some type of scam? Maybe she had some sort of fetish for prisoners that eased her pain over the loss of her husband—if that was even a true story. I wondered how many other prisoners she had contacted around the world before she hit on me. Was she playing some sort of numbers game until she found the perfect prisoner to prey upon? Was she searching for a replacement for her dead husband? And on and on . . . this is where my ego was taking me for my own protection.

It was only a few hours before the session's scheduled time of 9:30 PM Eastern time, and I was not in good shape. How could I possibly place my heart totally into this with all the doubt festering inside me? This would be like Arnold Palmer or Jack Nicklaus trying to focus on sinking a twelve-foot sliding, left-to-right putt just after drinking a fifth of bourbon. Was I nuts?

Suddenly a calm and quiet wave of peace passed through me, and my mind shifted over to the positive thoughts of Nakita's kind, sincere, humble, and encouraging letters, which had certainly indicated to me her involvement in all of this was truthful. And her knowledge of the *fifty principles* that are the foundation of *A Course in Miracles* was extremely convincing.

Being Alerted

By 7:30 PM, two hours before the session, many of my doubts had faded, and the ones that remained I could sense were soon to follow. I was resting flat on my back on my top bunk, wearing headphones and listening to a classic jazz radio station. This helped to drown out the obnoxious volume of constant bellowing, bickering, and just plain vulgar insanity in the housing unit. With 272 inmates, double-bunked and squeezed together within thirty inches of one another—this would be my haven where I would join in with the worldwide meditation/prayer session. There was no other place to physically move myself.

As I lay there on my rack, paging through a recent letter from my good friend Ron Skeen, which helped me to relax, I overheard a quiet conversation in the bunk area directly behind me. I was sure I heard the word "Croatia" mentioned, at least twice. Stunned, I removed my headphones to listen more attentively.

Sure enough, a few inmates had gathered in general conversation—"kicking it around" this is called. An inmate was telling another a story about his brother, who once spent some time during the 1990s in the country of Croatia while a war was going on. He talked about the crystal-clear water of the Adriatic Sea. He said that you could drop a coin in shoulder-deep water, and as it lay on the bottom you could read the print on the coin.

I am sure you will agree that Croatia is not a topic that we in this country often discuss in casual conversation. In fact, I'd had to use an atlas in the prison library to find its location when I first heard from Nakita. The country seems to wrap itself around Bosnia, just below Hungary and next to neighboring Serbia, across from Italy on the Adriatic Sea.

Regardless of the small talk in the discussion I overheard, my immediate thoughts were on the coincidence of this little-discussed nation coming up in a conversation here in prison. With less than two hours before the meditation was to begin, suddenly I was lit up. Was this really a coincidence? I asked myself. Or was this a signal of some sort, alerting me that I should trust in the validity of this whole affair? John Lennon once wrote a song about the kind of confusion I had experienced earlier in the day. Was his "Instant Karma" idea now telling me something I urgently needed to know? That we got what we put out, or what we mirror—could this be it?

I had no choice, as I saw it, but to quickly start thinking that this was intended to help me make a decision on not only the validity, but the value, of this worldwide meeting of minds. I was being guided to simply *let go* of any and all other negative thoughts. Even with that decision made, it was still difficult for me to not continue wondering about the number and identities of other individuals involved. Who were they? My guess was, I was not supposed to know.

One thing I do know, however, beyond any belief I could ever have, is that the Holy Spirit is the part of our minds that arbitrates between ego beliefs and our true essence or spirit. Always in favor of spirit, the Holy Spirit bridges the gap so that wrong-minded thinking will shift over to right-mindedness, which leads to our creativity. The Holy Spirit uses time in His task, so the process can occur in moments or can take much longer, depending on our individual willingness and readiness.

The ego believes this shift to knowledge to be a threat, as though something is being taken away. The ego is tough or stubborn in hanging onto old and ancient beliefs handed down over time. This is why the ego has a hard time trying to understand the *now*.

To our true spirit, however, the real essence of who we are, this shift is not seen as fearful or threatening. The shift is a necessary series of events, as long as we are here in the dream of time and form, and it does not need to be seen as threatening. With this Truth, our spirit will transcend into its own fullness and cannot conceive of excluding any part of its *being* from it.

So Why Was I Making Judgments?

Even with these good-minded thoughts and the alert signal from the Holy Spirit, I again regressed to vigilant questioning in my mind. This time it was over the time zones around the world. Why had Nakita scheduled this "meeting of minds" for 9:30 PM *Eastern* time, which was very convenient for me?

Again, positive right-minded thinking entered my mind, suggesting that maybe Nakita was not the organizer of this event. It was very possible it could have been arranged by, say, an individual or group in the Far East, or even Australia. Nakita never said she was the originator, so why was I hanging onto that notion?

Then it dawned on me like bright rays of sunlight bursting through cloud cover: Why should I be so concerned about all of this anyway? It really didn't matter who the organizer was or what time it occurred. With that one lasting thought I realized that time was only real in the Holy Spirit's use of it, and He was using it for this event.

Finally, I was urged by myself to simply let go of any negative-minded attempts to intrude on my thought process about this event, and I proceeded to set my sights on the peace I was feeling in general about the whole idea. Any wrong-minded thoughts from the ego would only block the extension of the thoughts from others, regardless of how many minds were involved. It would block my joy as well, which was really most important here for me to consider. If my own joy were to be blocked, then I would perceive myself as being unfulfilled. I went on to perceive this to be a necessary excitement for myself, here in prison, one that would give me a sense of accomplishment and completion, and most of all, wholeness.

What accomplishment do I mean? I'll let you answer that for yourself, while you contemplate the following passage from *A Course in Miracles*:

> Spirit knows that the awareness of all its brothers/sisters is included in its own, as it is included in God. The power of the whole Sonship and Its Creator is therefore spirit's own fullness, rendering its creations equally whole, and equal in perfection. The ego cannot prevail against a totality that includes God, and any totality must include God.

Chapter 39
The Bridge Club

Christopher Columbus yearned to look westward, one of the strongest insights of all time. He didn't carry around with him the reasoning taught by the world of his era and culture, that the world might be flat. Instead, he obeyed his intuition and an intent that refused to accept the world's fearful belief, and he convinced the queen of Spain to make a decision that allowed him to change history. The confusion over a flat world ended in an instant.

Whatever the decision is that we want to make, the inability or refusal to see the whole of it allows us to continue to think like the crowd. If your decision is from your heart but turns out to not be accurate, then it is not a loss at all because it is a right-minded error in perception, but blessed with *rightly intent* that will quickly be used by the Holy Spirit for a lesson yet to come.

In my own case over the meditation session, I was able to see my ego's stance against my participation as having no logical outcome. My ego's conclusion was it was an "idiotic idea" that I had bought into "from some lunatic" living in a foreign country. But with God, there are no conclusions because His will is continuous. Our own creations, if we must compare, are as close to a conclusion as we can fathom, but they carry on and never truly conclude.

God's thought established these creations in our minds right where they belong—in our mind rather than our body. Your identification with His mind is what gives you the state of mind of who you truly are. After all, the ego about you is not the real you. It's in your body that the ego-based beliefs carry on about your mind.

Your Willingness to See a Logical Outcome

We seem to accept into our split-mind that which is not really there, and deny what truly is. This keeps the mind continuing to fragment. You may deny the function God has given your mind through His mind, but you cannot prevent it. It is the logical outcome of what you are.

My ability to see a logical outcome in the matter of the meditation session depended on my willingness to see it. The factor of how many participants there would be had nothing to do with my own willingness to go forward. Whoever else would participate was already God's Will; I could not control or change that. But what I was able to affect was the result I could foresee within myself, by participating. God's Will was for me to participate regardless of how many others did so, and by denying that I would be denying my own true free will as well.

In the end I gladly participated in the meditation session, because a burning knowledge that lit up brightly inside me said that I must—a solid decision that helped me through the holidays here in prison. My restless mind became controlled and attained an energy that was truly mine. I held a great capacity for remaining calm and quiet. I felt as though I could concentrate on anything. For me that session was a real remedy for both healing and fulfillment with a great sense of harmony. The Christmas holidays came and went, and I really didn't dwell on it any longer. I continued to move forward in the daily regimen I set for myself, surviving in prison, writing this book and others, while seriously contemplating my release. I was due an early release, but when?

I did mail a short note to William, asking whether his sister had given him any word about the carbon copy flyer he had mailed her. I was also curious to know what part of New Mexico she lived in. I wanted to visualize in my mind exactly where this copy had finally settled down. I also decided to write to Nakita and let her know I did participate, but mostly I was concerned to know how she had come to write to me in the first place. Who gave her my information?

One thing for certain about William, he is always quick to reply to a letter from me in prison, and for good reason. He knows firsthand what being locked up as a prisoner is like. William understands the longing and the anxiety over receiving mail. And I enjoy his style of using a generic blank postcard to write back when only a few descriptive words and abbreviated sentences are necessary. If only there were more individuals in the world like William. He is unique, and certainly whole.

His reply indicated that he had spoken to his sister over the telephone just a few days prior to the meditation session. She told him that her card-playing bridge group had a game scheduled for the same night, and that the entire club of women were "spiritual seekers" or at least "curiosity seekers," and that on December 22 they would begin their time together by participating in the ten-minute session.

She was also aware that William had obtained the flyer from his friend in prison—me. This made it more interesting when informing the other women in the bridge club. William's sister said she had made a photocopy of the flyer for herself as a memento, and for possible future use, and then mailed the original carbon copy to her friend in another state. She felt giving her friend the actual carbon copy would add "an effect," being that it was put together in prison by an inmate and a friend of her own brother. She thought her friend would appreciate its value.

It appeared her out-of-state friend also had a group get-together, a holiday party of some sort, on that same evening. She supposedly introduced the flyer to the group for their participation at the exact time specified. William said his sister was thrilled to have a sense of belonging to something good-hearted. He hadn't heard more from her on the subject. William is a quiet individual who will simply let his sister inform him when the time is right.

As I placed William's postcard into my footlocker, I couldn't help but to experience a joyful thrill with a slight chuckle, and continued to smile over this news for the entire night. At least now I was aware that I was not alone that evening during those ten minutes of "mind gathering." This was enough for me to settle down on the matter and move forward with my thoughts. The recurrent thought that now obsessed me was: "I gotta get out of this place." But another thought always seemed to blanket that thought: "You're okay. You'll make it. Just keep doing what you're doing."

God's Will Is Not Our Wish

If you will accept that the Holy Spirit will direct you, as He did here with me, you can realize it in a way so as to avoid pain. Surely no one in their right-mind could object to this goal if you were aware of it when it's taking place. Being aware of it depends on whether or not you truly want to listen to what He is teaching you. We never know what He has in mind for us in His Reasoning, although we can be certain that ultimately it involves our healing.

We know more about healing as we heal. We no more recognize what is painful than we know what is joyful and are, in fact, very apt to confuse the two. The Holy Spirit's main lesson is teaching us to tell them apart. Here's what I mean:

Many believe that whatever is joyful "now" will cost in the end. Or that we must first pay or sacrifice to attain joy. The thinking seems to be "What goes up must come down." This leads some people to drugs or alcohol, to mention a few, so that they may control their own wishes as to when they may experience a high. As long as we're in doubt about what or who we are, we will remain confused about pain and joy.

This confusion is what inspired the whole idea of sacrifice. By placing the weight of our pain on sacrificing, we believe we make the pain a "smaller pill to swallow." But as we listen to the Holy Spirit we are giving up the ego. Remember, we learned earlier that there are only two thought systems. One is the illusory, ego-based mind, and the other is real and communicated to us by the Holy Spirit of God. In His communication within total oneness of all that exists, there is no requirement for sacrifice. How could there be, unless you're dreaming of duality? In understanding this you are conflict-free.

This is why we need to begin demonstrating the obvious to ourselves, though it has not always been obvious to us. If you believe that doing the opposite of God's Will can be better for you, then you will strengthen your beliefs that it is possible to actually succeed in the opposite of His Will. This is the karma you will make. You'll discover sooner or later that this is insane and will drive you deeper into insanity. You would be trying to believe that an impossible choice is open to you—one that is both fearful and desirable.

We must remember, "God Wills," He does not make wishes come true. What is true always has been true. Your *will* is as powerful as His because it *is* His. The ego's wishes mean nothing because the ego always wishes for the truly impossible. You can wish all you want for the impossible, and you will get nothing. But if you "will" it, along with God in oneness, you will have what it is you want. There will be *needs* along the way, and you'll have them met too. Your knowledge of this is your strength, which weakens the ego.

Your Trustworthiness

Now that you know where your strength comes from, also know that the Holy Spirit always sides with it. This adds strength. But if you avoid His Guidance, you'll only be asking for weakness.

Let's face it, being weak is frightening. If this is your decision, then you must want to be afraid. The Holy Spirit will never guide you toward sacrifice. But the ego will try to convince you that sacrifice is your "strong arm" against fear. When you are confused about this type of motivation, it's due to the images you are projecting. Notice how you feel when you are confused or resistant for change, and just decide this is not the time to be feeling this way. This confusion makes trust impossible.

No one will honor a guide he or she doesn't trust. But this doesn't mean the guide is untrustworthy. However, the follower of this guide may be. This too is merely a matter of the follower's own belief.

Look at it this way: If you believe you can betray, you will believe that everything is capable of betraying you. Yet this is only because you elected to follow false guidance. Unable now to further follow this guidance without fear, you associate fear with guidance, and refuse to follow any guidance at all. No wonder the result of a decision can be confusing. So when we want to change a condition, we need to say something like this: "I am willing to release this pattern within me that is making this condition."

The Holy Spirit is as trustworthy as you are, because He is you. Your trustworthiness is beyond question, but the ego's is questionable. Your trustworthiness will always remain solid, no matter how you question it. We've learned so far that you and I and everyone else are the Will of God. His Will is an optional choice only to the ego which doesn't really exist, since what we are *is* what we truly are.

The entire idea as a whole, of the separation, back to the symbolic Garden of Eden, lies in this error. The only way out of this error is to decide you don't have to decide on anything any longer. You are what you are by God's decision. He decided about you based on His idea of you, regardless of how you dream. You cannot undo this.

Even when we make a false decision based on fantasy, and then turn around to relinquish it, which drives the ego into more worry and fear, the relinquishment decision is not a wish. It is accomplished by the Will of God, who stands firm behind you, around you, and within you.

His voice, which is communicated to you from within, will teach you how to distinguish between pain and joy. God's voice is your true *intent* and is what will guide you out of any confusion you may have made for yourself.

Chapter 40
Your Natural Environment

If you are one of those who believe they are only their body and that the body is where it all ends, then you probably would not have read this far into this book. Since you are reading this, it most likely means that you have had at least a glimpse of something beyond your flesh and bones. Regardless of your beliefs, please answer to yourself a question that once consumed many others at some point in their lives, who have been responsible for major breakthroughs that positively changed the face of humanity.

Have you ever felt at any particular time you were guided to make a breakthrough decision? Whether it be with family, career, social, or any other obligation, most of us at one time or another have had to make a serious decision.

The decision was also most likely made easily and with minimal doubt. Even when doubts seemingly did weigh heavy, you knew the choice you were going to make, regardless of doubt and fear. Following the Holy Spirit is natural and therefore is easy. The world seems to *work* against nature. I use the word "work" because going against your natural tendency is always *work*.

The *Course* teaches us in more ways than you may think that there are "no orders of difficulty in miracles," yet the world perceives orders of difficulty in everything. This is because the ego cannot understand the concept of wholly desirable. But many are gaining the knowledge that anything within themselves that operates out of wholeness has not one thing more difficult than another. I'm sure you know within yourself that there is no difficulty at all when you operate from your natural state. This is your state of grace.

Every Son of God has this natural state; otherwise, a person is out of his or her natural environment and therefore cannot function well. Have you ever felt your pursuit in any given situation to be a strain? Of course, we all have. This is when you are operating against your naturalness. There's no point in pushing harder. The situation may budge, but will end up in turmoil. The only environment where you will not experience strain is being where you belong. Where you belong is the only environment you're worthy of, because your worth is beyond anything you can make.

Cocreating with Truth

Consider where you are right now. I'm not talking about your physical surroundings; I mean the kingdom you have made. Can you honestly judge its worth? Is your chosen kingdom where you will have the natural ability to experience joy, eternally? If so, then it is a place where peace is protected from conflict and your heart untouched by fear or loss. You cannot manufacture or construct this place, or anything like it, any more than you can *make* yourself. This place of the "natural you" was created for you along with you; yet you deny it.

Your mind is light, the same light as my mind, and we both only know light. Our knowledge is nowhere else. Your radiance extends to attract the darkness of other minds, who at first may be startled or frightened. God gives equally, and when you have recognized the light in anyone, you have acknowledged it in yourself. Your only difficulty is in the way you trained yourself.

While you are out of your natural environment you might ask yourself, "What really is Truth?" This is when you don't know yourself. The Truth includes all of the Sons of God, your brothers and sisters, the Sonship, which is the wholeness of Truth. Without Truth God does not exist, and this certainly is not the case. How can we be sure of this? Let's answer this by asking, How else could we have arrived, or even have chosen to separate from the Truth that created us? We either make a way for ourselves or we cocreate within this Truth, called God.

Remember, we learned earlier that the Kingdom is forever extending within its already-infiniteness, as the Mind of God. When you're not experiencing your own joy, or the capability you have for this elation, it's because you don't have the knowledge of your own self-fullness. By not knowing this self-fullness you are excluding part of Heaven from yourself, and therefore are not whole.

When a split-mind fragments with its ego-based beliefs, and cannot perceive its fullness, it needs a miracle. What is the miracle? It is your wholeness creating a new vision upon what you think is your deprived mind, restoring it to Heaven—but only if you're able to accept this wholeness as real. This part of you is Heaven. It is in full appreciation of its fullness, where selfishness is impossible, leaving only room for extension. Therefore, what appreciates grows in strength, and that is why true strength is always peaceful. When you are fulfilled you are operating by your true spirit. Your creativity comes alive, because the Holy Spirit, who is in your mind, knows your creations as your purpose. He will bring them into your awareness if you'll let Him. Your creations are part of your true essence or being and are what fulfills you. The creations of the entire Sonship are yours as well, since every creation is of this wholeness, and they belong to everyone. This is why we are all abundant.

The Wine Tasting

Abundance came alive for me a few days after receiving William's postcard, informing me of his sister's involvement in the worldwide meditation and how she had sent the carbon copy to her friend in a different state. That message itself was still sinking in when another letter showed up for me from the wine country out in California. It was from Jon Phillips, my long-ago golf pal from Florida who was now living out west near the vineyards. Needless to say, it was a huge thrill to hear from him again, and so soon.

The very first line of his extremely exciting letter went like this: "Hello Jim. How on earth did you figure out a way to come alive at a wine-tasting party that Becky and I went to recently?"

His first several words surely threw me for a loop, but I sensed something good to come and was eager to read on. I remembered Becky, Jon's wife, from our Florida days, and her involvement with yoga. I also recalled how Jon would use yoga strategies for mind-quieting to help his golf game.

Jon proceeded to tell me about a private wine-tasting gathering hosted by Becky's yoga club as a Christmas party. There were eighteen people there on December 22, the same night as the meditation session, which I had already put behind me. The yoga club had invited a wine expert to bring in several wines from around the world, in addition to California wines. Everyone in the group brought a covered dish that would complement good wine, and Becky made her famous crabmeat and artichoke dip, which I remembered well.

Jon said when they arrived at the party, there was a lovely middle-aged woman, elegantly dressed, softly playing the violin, accompanied by a man in a tuxedo on piano. Each individual was handed a flyer about a meditation for world peace to begin at 6:30 PM (9:30 PM Eastern time). My eyes flew wide open at what I was reading.

Jon said the first thing to catch his eye on the flyer threw him almost into shock. Ecstatic, he didn't know what to think as he stared directly at my name and prison address centered at the top of the flyer. He pointed this out to Becky, and they gazed at it in awe.

Jon asked Becky to see what she could find out from Reba, an older woman and the leader of the group. He said his first thought was it must be a prank, but immediately dismissed that thought, as he knew I was in prison. Then he said that he knew that whatever was happening, it had to be good.

Credit Due to Reba

The wine-tasting party began at 5:30 PM Pacific time, with plans to stop whatever they were doing to join in the worldwide meditation at 6:30. This gave Jon an hour to mingle and find out what he could. "Why was Jim's name on that flyer?" he asked everyone, persisting to point at what was by now a raggedy and worn carbon copy.

As it turned out, Becky's yoga friend Reba had organized the flyer part of the party. She admitted she didn't know me, but bragged that her friend who lived in New Mexico had a brother in Ohio who had spent time in prison. Reba said that her friend's brother (William) still corresponded with the author of the carbon copy, who was still an inmate.

Suddenly in everyone's mind I was the one who dreamed up this idea. Of course, no one was aware of Nakita's involvement and whoever else preceded her. Reba, a good-natured hostess, proudly explained to everyone that her friend mailed her the carbon copy, which was the actual copy that came directly from inside the penitentiary—thus my handwriting. Reba had taken it upon herself to make new photocopies on quality paper so that each person at the party could have a memento. Jon said, "Reba took this to heart and had fun with it."

Jon described to me how, as he stood there in amazement, staring at the flyer, he could not help but picture me at that very moment, behind bars in Ohio, getting ready to participate in this event. He envisioned me at my bunk, at the same time he and Becky and the rest of the group of wine tasters, and God knows who else from around the world, would be joining together in peace. He said the entire yoga club Becky belongs to was highly enthused over the idea.

Jon said, as he stared at my handwriting on the carbon copy, that he thought back to the times in Florida when we played serious golf together. He also thought about many of the deep conversations we'd had on topics such as world hunger, the homeless, God, Heaven, women, sports, our children, and more. He thought about my three daughters, wondering how they were doing with me being in prison. The last time I had seen Jon, my youngest daughter was only one year old.

Jon admitted that joyful tears came to his eyes as Becky gave him a long hug. He said they both looked at each other smiling, and accepting in a truly strong, positive way that I was with them that evening.

Of course, the word at the wine-tasting party circulated instantly that Jon was close friends with me, and also that neither of us had planned this incident in any fashion. The credit here was certainly due to Reba, who had no clue that anyone in the group would possibly have a friend in Ohio who was in prison.

In fact, the startling coincidence mesmerized the entire group, and a particular, unmistakable joy became present, as the eighteen of them, plus the pianist, the violinist, and the wine expert, gathered in a circle holding hands at precisely 6:30 PM. At the same time, I was lying on my back on my top bunk, surrounded by prison noise and chaos, and for ten minutes, to help world peace, our radiance extended these words:

Peace be to me, the holy Son of God.
Peace to my brothers and sisters who are one with me.
Let all the world be blessed with peace through us.

Jon added that the wine tasted extremely fine that evening, and also that it was a safe party, with no one making the error of overindulging. He said that the entire evening the others were asking about me, and Jon shared many of our golf stories—the good, the bad, and the ugly rounds of golf. He added that Reba, the organizer, who seemed to glow with a radiant light, suggested that everyone feel free to use the flyer she had copied, inserting their own names, for any future meditation they may want to organize, big or small.

Jon said that during the small talk, someone said they had heard on the national news that due to a severe financial crisis, Ohio was not the only state making huge cuts in their prison system budget. The news suggested prison closings and the release of many nonviolent cases. Jon asked that I hang tough—that prayers from many were being extended so that freedom would ring for me soon.

The Carbon Copy Toasted

All of this, from Nakita in Croatia to Jon and his friends in the wine country, and all the others, caused me to reflect on a lesson in *A Course in Miracles*: "The miracle is a lesson in total perception. By including any part of totality in the lesson, you have included the whole."

In the closing of Jon's lengthy letter, he made a point that this had certainly created a special holiday for him and that he was aware I had no idea of how deeply his thoughts were with me at the wine-tasting party. He said that Becky could not wait to give me a hug.

Jon also told me of a few specific individuals, as well as the whole group together, toasting me several times as they raised their wine glasses toward their flyers. Then, he said, they all started to laugh over this whole possibility.

Jon and Becky were soon to be off on a ski vacation they had planned for several months. He said they were going to a ski resort that neither of them had heard of before and would write me in detail upon their return. But better yet, maybe I would be released from prison soon and could sit down in person with the two of them. I was deeply touched.

As I set his letter down next to me where I lay on my bunk, settling my head back to regroup a bit, I couldn't help the flow of tears that poured down my face. A warm, sort of tingling sensation swept through my body like an ocean wave, and I felt a wonderful glow with a comfortable smile become *of* me. It was God, and with no thought of letters in the alphabet with space between them.

I had an overabundance of joy and much to be thankful for. This fullness I was feeling could not be contained or locked up behind bars. It was intended to extend inward to the whole Sonship. My tears were expressing a confidence of a knowing I indeed had of myself, and what it was I was meant to do, and be.

PART VI
BEYOND THE EGO

Chapter 41
There is No Substitute

The fear of God has become what we think to be our reality. We try not to even begin to realize the magnitude of that one error—the "original sin" of the separated ego, or the symbolic situation in which Eve projected the serpent luring her to eat the so-called forbidden fruit, in turn causing Adam to panic and try to cover up the matter, sending both of them into a lifetime of guilt. Humanity has been fearful of the "Tree of Knowledge" ever since.

The error was so vast and so completely incredible that from it a world of total unreality was made. The emergence of that one *substituted* thought—the thought of the separated ego substituted for the truth of Oneness—is to this day what we think we live inside of. We're bounced around in its fragmentation, a motion that continues to add more fear.

Additionally, we refuse to realize that this event, bringing us into the dream world of time, space, and form, was only an error in thought—an error that can be simply undone or reversed. But there is nothing in that error that will truly keep us from experiencing Heaven. We only choose to think so, because of guilt and fear. What can it possibly be that brings about our disunited perceptions, forcing us to make continuous substitutions for Truth? The fear of God, or fear of True Reality, is the only cause of this insane problem.

From the moment of the first separation, the images of our errors are projected outward. The world we physically see in all its forms, shapes, and sizes, colors, even fragrances, arose in the ever-fragmenting and substituting split-mind.

The movie screen, so to speak, on which these projections portray its images is passed along from generation to generation, which in true reality is only a blink or flicker of the eyelid. What we're afraid to realize is that if we take away the projection and look behind the screen, we will find ourselves naked in truth. Truth extends infinitely inward, where the idea of loss is meaningless.

Truth Won't Desert You

Isn't it strange that a world that cannot find lasting peace, where everything is in chaos attack, and defense, arose from this projection—the original separation from the One-Mind of God, a separation that formed the illusive ego-based mind? When you are able to bring truth to this, you will know the reality that lies within, and in quietness will take no part in these insane projections any longer.

But in order to do so, let's not place guilt on ourselves, because the past is only the images on the movie screen, and does not really exist. Only behind the screen is true reality. Besides, guilt implies the past occurred. More importantly we must not be afraid of the truth, or we are merely believing in what doesn't exist. This will only guarantee more fear and continued fragmentation.

When you are confronted with this insane form of the original error rising to frighten you, simply say to yourself this quick prayer:

God is not fear, but He is Love.

This will help you to see how ridiculous fear really is. We can say this is what is really meant by "The truth will save you" or "The truth will set you free."

Truth as you possess it will never desert you; so you do not need this insane world giving you substitutions. Inward is where your sanity abides, and every ounce of insanity is outside of you. If you believe that truth is found outside of you, and that error and guilt are within, you cannot help but be a body of substitution without an ounce of substance.

The *Course* paints us an elegant tapestry of senseless substitutions that are touched with insanity, and it looks like this:

Your substitutions are swirling lightly on a mad course like feathers dancing insanely in the wind with no substance. They fuse and merge and separate, in shifting and totally meaningless patterns that need not be judged at all. To judge them individually is pointless. Their tiny difference in form are not real difference at all; none of them matter.

Let them all go, dancing in the wind, dipping and turning till they disappear from sight, far, far, outside of you. And turn you to the stately quiet and calm within, where in holy stillness dwells the living God you never had, and retraces with your mad journey outside yourself, leading you gently back to truth and safety within.

Your Holy Ground

You can count on the Holy Spirit bringing all your insane projections and wild substitutions, which you've placed outside yourself, to the truth. It is the truth of who and what you are, with no need of substitution, that restores you to reason and allows you to see the error of that illusion as unreal. Go ahead, right now: Take a look at yourself. You won't see yourself outside anywhere, unless it is a projection or a reflection.

Even in your relationships, where the Holy Spirit has taken charge of everything, He has set the pathway for you to go inward to the truth you share with these individuals. If the relationship is based on images, sooner or later the projection will end. In the insane world outside of you, nothing is shared and is always substituted, and sharing and substituting have nothing in common in the real world. Within yourself is the real world, and the oneness you share with your brothers/sisters. Here, nothing is projected.

This place where you know the truth to be is your *holy ground*, where substitutes are unheard of. This holy ground, as translated by the Holy Spirit, is where you are joined with your Creator, your Source of life. That original error has never been a threat to your own holiness, nor ever will be.

In this place of holiness that is your reality, the real you, is the radiant light of Truth in which the Holy Spirit has committed your relationships. So allow Him to bring the relationship here, where it can be real. Just give Him the truth by showing no need for substitutes. That of which is truly within you, the substance of who you are, or Heaven, has not a single substitute.

Within each of us, separation is truly nonexistent, where separation is not possible. The reality of you and me, along with everyone else, is God's One Creation. It is not split apart into fragments. Separation is made, not created.

It's this simple: We are firmly joined in truth that can only be of God, and God certainly doesn't make errors. But He does understand that very first error that built all other errors, and it's okay. The reason it is okay is that God doesn't accept a substitute in place of you, because it wouldn't be real. He doesn't even see it because it's an illusion you made. God has overlooked this illusion by only seeing you as beyond it, which is forgiveness. His Thought beyond our illusions is what holds His One Creation together.

Our relationships with one another within this One Thought of God are whole, and beautiful, and truthful. This is safety, and all illusions are gently brought to the truth, where they simply fade away. This is how you feel in Truth. Isn't it a strength so powerful you can't describe it? This is the Universe within each of us standing as one. It is Heaven, and there is no substitute.

Chapter 42
The Evolving of Holiness

In his book *Journey to Ixtlan*, Carlos Castaneda describes his teacher carefully instructing and reminding him about the fine art of dreaming: "Every time you look at anything in your dreams it changes shapes." There seems to be a tendency to either merge with the dream figures, which constantly keeps pulling one back into the dream plot, or to move toward wakefulness. But there have always been those who are able to maintain a fine balance between wakefulness and sleep. If this is the case, however, are you able to distinguish between yourself and dream images?

Think about where our minds must be when we dream. During these moments that a dream takes place, don't we see a world that seems real? Think about those characters and situations that are of your choosing. Doesn't the dream seem to be totally out of proportion to the world? Our own fascinations bring us what we thought was out of reach and change to satisfy the ego. We would not need to have dreams if we didn't see ourselves as needing the ego, and always feeling as though we are under attack by someone or something ready to deprive us.

Our dreams have no concern with what is true, and our conflicting wishes, wants, and needs bring chaos and misunderstanding to what we dream. A dream is the best example of how we form our perceptions—illusion as a substitute for the truth. But when we wake from our sleep we don't take the dream seriously, because we see that we remain safe in reality.

Dreams are a way of looking at the world and changing it to better suit our egos. Dreams are excellent examples both of the ego's inability to tolerate true reality and our willingness to change reality on the ego's behalf.

Making a World in Dreams

We may not find what we see while in sleeping dreams versus when awake, because what we see in our waking life we blot out in our dreams. We arrange everything in dreams. People become what we want them to be, and we direct what they do. There are no limits in our substitutes. For a while it seems as if the world were given to us to make as we wish. But we're really trying to attack the world, trying to defeat it and make it serve us.

When we consider this, couldn't we conclude that dreams are ongoing temper tantrums in which we make our demands? It's no different than a child who screams, "I want this toy now!"

However, the dream does not have an origin that will allow us to escape. Anger and fear seem to spread throughout it, and in an instant the illusion of satisfaction is invaded by the illusion of terror.

We often dream of our ability to control reality by substituting a world that we prefer, rather than the waking world that can be terrifying. We know that our attempts to blot out reality are frightening, but we're not willing to admit it. Therefore, we substitute the fantasy of reality being fearful, rather than simply live in reality. By labeling it fearful, we have an excuse. Of course, then we make more excuses to cover our fear and guilt. This is the ego at work, splitting and fragmenting more thought.

For myself, it always seemed that my dreams were showing me I had the power to make a world as I'd like to see it. While I was seeing it, I surely didn't doubt whether it was real or not. It seemed real, and yet this dream was a world only in my mind that seemed to be outside of me. We don't respond to our dreams as though we made them, nor do we realize that the emotions the dream produces must come from us.

It's the figures in the dreams and their actions that seem to make the dream. We really don't realize that we are actually making them act out for us. But if we did realize this, we would see they have no guilt. Why is this? Because they're not real. The illusion of satisfaction of the dream figure is also not there. We wake up, and the dream figures, as well as the dream itself, have left us. But we fail to recognize that what caused the dream remains with us.

It's the wish to make another world that remains in all of us. What we seem to awaken to is another form of this same unreal world that we see in dreams. All of our time is spent dreaming. Our sleeping and our waking dreams have different forms, but that is the only difference. Their content is the same.

Dreams are our protest against reality, and our fixed and insane idea that we can change it. Why do we wish to change it? Because it frightens us. Why does reality frighten us? Because deep within we know true reality is of God, and we think we fear Him.

From Special to Holy in Relationships

In our ego-based dream of life we make special relationships that have a special place outside of our divine Reality. They are special because we "made" them, as though to make a reality of them. This is the means by which we try to make all of our dreams come true.

From this special thought of a special relationship, we don't awaken. These special relationships are our determination to keep our hold on the unreal, and to prevent ourselves from truly awakening to the naked truth behind the projection screen. We see more value in sleeping than in waking, so we hide from reality. However, there are special relationships in which the holiness in each other seems to unite and leads us from our sleep. This becomes a "holy relationship" and is real and necessary to discover and bring forward true peace and joy.

The Relationship Shift

The Holy Spirit, who certainly has the wisdom of our dreams—from our simple daydreams and imaginings to the complicated or restless dreams as we sleep—uses all of them as means for awakening from the dream humanity dreams.

The Holy Spirit is constantly undoing the errors, leading us to happy dreams. Happy dreams are a necessary step toward no longer fearing God. The fear must be released in order to awaken wholly, and this step cannot be achieved through unhappy dreams. This is the Holy Spirit's task before dreams can disappear. The dream of separation that humanity dreams is no different, and when it finally fades away we will have awakened at Home, where we've always been.

But we must first release ourselves from the fear of God as a whole before we may awaken as a whole. This is exactly what the Holy Spirit is doing in His use of the special relationship. He is sorting out and sorting through to find where holiness might unite.

In some cases, a holy relationship will result, either directly or indirectly, and in some cases will not. He does not destroy nor take a special relationship away from us, but He does use each one differently, as a help in making His purpose real to you. As the special relationship's unholy aspect keeps it a thing apart or separate, its holiness aspect hidden within it will gradually come forward and become an offering to everyone.

The Holy Spirit proceeds with your special relationships while shifting them to holy relationships, those you will share with all you encounter. This is why we have been returning throughout this book to the importance of love bringing forward joy. When we extend, we bring love/joy forward in the mind.

Your joy keeps you in a happy dream. Your blessings of right-mindedness continually extend. Don't think the Holy Spirit has forgotten anyone in the purpose He has given us. And don't think He has forgotten you, to whom He gave the gift. He uses everyone as a means for the awakening of everyone. He has set His goal on awakening all of us through each other. So give all of your special relationships to His care.

How do you know which relationships are *special* and which ones are *holy*? That's quite easy. Where holiness abides, it does not feel lacking. All of this is exactly the thought process I decided to institute upon receiving another letter from Nakita in Croatia.

Hearing from Nakita Again

Nakita's next letter to me showed up in January at Hocking Prison, where I had recently been transferred. This transfer was an overdue break from the "Gladiator Camp" of Belmont Prison, where the average age range of the inmates is eighteen to twenty-eight years old, and death and violence were all-pervasive. For me this transfer felt like still being at war, but transferred off the front lines.

At Hocking I now lived among a group of prisoners mostly aged fifty or more. Many of these men had been incarcerated for much of their adult lives. One man in particular, who was seventy-eight years old, had first entered an Ohio prison in 1958 and had not left prison since. Now that I was in a somewhat more relaxed environment, I found myself more willing to help those older than myself, rather than feeling forced to focus my thoughts and energy in constant self-defense mode against young gladiators, as I had faced at Belmont.

I was thrilled to receive another letter from Nakita; I had wondered whether I would ever hear from her again. I still didn't know what to think of her intentions toward me, but I sensed her to be a great individual, and I felt no threat in any way.

Before I expand a bit on her letter to me, I'd like to share with you the exact wording of her opening lines, just to give you a taste of her Croatian tongue, translated by her to English.

Dearest Jim,

Peace for you with blessings. I hope you done the meditation on 22 December. I have 12 people and myself on back lawn at my farm. We done candles with sky filled. It was lovely and we pray for you too. My friends ask why your country require prison for you for such insane matter. Juno, my friend in Philippines, came back home now for a while. He say he had a group there to do meditation with that night. This is how he show me about it and I show you...

I will write again when I return from trip to Boston. I hope to see you out of prison soon.

Making Sense

Nakita's letter continued at length. She indicated that another of her friends, Milan, also of Croatia, was spending much time in the Philippines for his job. This is where he met a group of individuals who led him to the worldwide meditation. He, in turn, sent the information to Nakita, who sent it to me, and I've already described how the carbon copy I made found its way to a wine-tasting party in the Sonoma Valley of California—among God only knows where else.

Just from this small sampling I could see that many others must have been involved from all around the world, though most likely the mystery will remain as to how many, who, or where.

Nakita went on to tell me that she was on her way to Boston for an important meeting regarding a project pertaining to her farmland in the hills outside the Croatian city of Split. Her plans involved using the land for a purpose that will bring people joy. She didn't provide specifics, but I sensed an excitement in her words about her trip to the United States.

She continued in an enthusiastic tone about an Internet search she had done. She discovered a few websites with newspaper articles about Ohio's financial crisis. She said among other efforts to cut expenditures from Ohio's budget was a severe slashing of the prison system. It seems a poll of Ohio voters had shown the people were favorably behind the new governor's goal of total prison reform, including the laws on sentencing of nonviolent cases and much more. She added that her Internet search was proof enough that Ohio, as well as some other states, had built a monster of a prison system that has grown financially out of control. Many individuals had been imprisoned, when alternative measures could have been taken.

Nakita commented, "It is too sad that your country had to experience rough financial times in order to realize that imprisoning decent people who made simple errors is not the right-minded approach to much of this nation's problems."

Of course, through the limited newspaper and television news that we do receive in prison, I was already aware of some of the information Nakita was feeding me. But I found her enthusiasm over this to be encouraging.

Also, this showed me that I had *somehow* gained a new friend. This relationship was evolving quickly, and I had not even physically met this lovely woman. Whether further evolution and good—or let me say holiness—will come of this, I have left in the realm of the Holy Spirit. Something was brewing, and I felt a certain peace in her kindness, that seemed to be a shining light on a destiny hidden within the words of her handwritten letters to me.

Chapter 43
Reality Holds Your Holiness

Consider the unreality we live among each day, and that of past generations, and those yet to arrive. The fake or phony ways we believe we are helping others, trying to impress the world, and of course our own egos, only make a stronger projection of a world gone mad.

We seem to walk the way of dreams through each day and usually each moment of each day. We are consistently learning to see illusion instead of Truth, fantasy over reality, going from waking to sleeping and on to a yet deeper dream. The illusions we make sink us deeper into the dream of separation.

Each dream we have within the dream of life, time, and space leads us to other dreams, and every fantasy that seems to offer us light only leads to further darkness. The vicious cycle of fragmenting continues, dream to dream, fantasy to fantasy, more illusion, on and on.

When I look back it seems that for me, the goal was also a search for the light that would end all frustration. But darkness remained, while a single ray of natural light just seemed unable to illumine my path. It was blocked. The dark area was incomplete, but enough for me to hide behind. But what was I hiding from? Could it be the truth about my real self?

The insanity of the world was always available to welcome me, but it was as though I felt I owed it something or had to please it. I had to learn quickly that the light I was working at hiding is my reality. I knew that if I didn't learn soon that darkness can only cover my light, and not put it out, I would be lost permanently to the insanity the world lives by. The light is *who* and *what* we are, regardless of the world's view.

Sure, the darkness at times still may make me feel weary and uncertain, especially now, as I think I can sense my incarceration period coming to an end. But the light always brings me back to the alertness of who I am. Thoughts that are not so pure penetrate often, but my own right-mindedness has learned to quickly come to the rescue, offering sane thoughts of love for myself and the whole.

It seemed that before, as the light would come closer or become brighter, I'd often fear it, or want to cool it down or dim its brilliance, so some darkness or a little bit of wrong-mindedness could reenter and give me some familiarity. But the dark thoughts, regardless of their temporary comfort, would shrink me away from truth, and the fear would continue— usually with a "doom and gloom" attitude taking over.

When we experience this type of seeming setback, however, we are still advancing, because our natural goal is to advance, away from fear and toward truth. We find it difficult to admit sometimes, but the truth gives us a sense of security from the dark. We try not to realize it by not accepting the knowledge we have within us of the truth. If we will accept this knowledge of the truth of who we are, the knowledge alone will drive us out of fear, and then signify a willingness to learn more. To learn more we must trust the *Light of Truth*.

Developing a Sense of No Fear

When I first entered prison my way of "taking the bull by the horns" was to ask myself what seemed to be frightening: "What is the worst thing that can possibly happen to me?"

After carefully considering this, I accepted the fact that I could possibly be killed in a number of violent ways. Facing this kept me from stepping backward, deeper into fear. This truth alone allowed my fear to wade in shallow water. This helped with a clear decision as to how I would carry myself in the event I was approached in a violent manner.

Of course, this most inevitable showdown did present itself, many times, in the early stages of my prison confinement, and the threat still does hang in the air to this day, but with minimal action. My method, instilled in me *somehow*, is to stand there, face to face with the individual and with no weapon of my own, such as the commonly used shank. My eye contact has always assured the culprit that I want no trouble; however, I am ready to handle myself physically if I must. Usually the result has been the confrontation ending in some sort of peaceful resolve. Unfortunately, there was an incident where dodging a shank did get me a mop handle slammed into my ribcage, from which I suffered bruised ribs that took six months to heal. Another event resulted in stitches in the back of my head.

But the truth I decided to live with was that if I were to be seriously hurt, disabled, or killed—which, by the way, does happen more than just occasionally—I would still be who I am while living in eternity. This attitude may seem unlikely, but if you were ever faced with this, with nowhere to run and hide, you would have no choice but to make some serious decisions in preparation for eventualities.

I was able, *somehow*, automatically it seemed, to develop a sense of no fear of losing my body to any such fate. Routinely I would ask myself, "What is the worst thing that can happen to me?" Then I would live out my days in that thought. This type of quickly learned faith has shown me an *intelligence* that cannot be topped. This may seem to you some sort of brave front I have been wearing as a denial of possible death. It sure is, but only to the ego.

I can tell you that from my own experiences here in prison, if we merely ask for truth to come and meet us, it will come in an instant. When we really know in a personal way of the light within us, shining bright as we travel our path, fear is impossible. But so often we refuse this knowledge, and this is the denial.

The dream of darkness has been so misleadingly cruel, and we're all deep into it as a whole. Thus fear restricts our eyes from opening long enough from our dream state to allow the light to permeate.

A Course in Miracles expresses this ever so poignantly: "A little flicker of your eyelids, closed for so long, has not been sufficient to give you confidence in yourself, so long despised."

Sharing the Fearless Truth

Think about the ways we walk toward love as we look for it, still hating it and terribly afraid of how it may treat us. Or are we really afraid of what we are capable of making of it, or *creating* of it?

Answering this question within yourself can be an advancement to love's meaning and a way to leave behind the illusions that have you surrounded. But if we revert to illusion, our fears increase. Let's be real here for a moment. Don't you really know the truth about yourself, and isn't it solid in rock, rather than of sand?

When we are able to share the fearless truth with a brother/sister who may be frightened, we are holding his/her hand in the chain of Atonement. With this chain of minds linked together, we can confidently say this is our connection or our link with Jesus, our model for One-mindedness and our elder brother leading the way in the reawakening process. Jesus entered the dream for the purpose of resurrecting as Christ, which gave us the direction for our own awakening.

But remember, Jesus was able to manifest the Holy Spirit through Right-mindedness, on to One-mindedness, where He experienced himself as Christ. He shows us the same path with the same ability He had while on this earth—or I should say, while living among us in the dream of separation.

Also keep in mind that the period from His birth to bodily death to the present day, which we call two thousand years of time, is only an instant or less, as time is only of the dream. In reality, behind the projection screen, time does not exist. But the Holy Spirit uses time while we dream, for the process of reawakening.

Jesus lives on in the Christ-Mind and is at the beginning of the Atonement procession line, leading us to the altar where we awaken as a whole. The altar is where God stands as One-Mind for us to awaken to and realize. Right now the Oneness of Mind surely is there; it's just that part of it sleeps.

It's when we lose our faith in this process that we slip back into darkness. This occurs due to our bodily focus—in other words, our unwillingness to look beyond—and the result is the projection of the body as who we are. The bodily image allows us to temporarily remain a projection.

When we can learn to see beyond this projection without fear, we see Christ in ourselves. This is our holiness. It only requires our desire for the truth of who we are. Let me ask you one question. Truthfully, now: How do you see yourself?

The Desire for Truth

Each instant we spend seeing ourselves as united with the interlocking chain of minds enables us to see our desired goals while in this world as fully attainable. These instants will strengthen the desire to reach our goals, if they are real, because achieving them is part of the Holy Spirit's use of time for His completion plans for the awakened chain.

Try to see that your own desired goals are those of your true free will, which is God's purpose for you. It has already been charted out, and all you need to do is not be afraid of the light and act by truth. This is what will direct you.

With this, you can tell yourself that you are the "bringer of salvation" and therefore have a function in this world of bringing light to darkness. The darkness in you is being brought to light as you read this book, among many other things you are being led to. You will be made whole with your desire to make whole.

The difficulty in all of this for me has always been my worry of not having enough time. However, I didn't realize that all the fear I had ever experienced was always due to this "time dilemma"—my fears of the future even more than my regrets over the past.

Now I am able to consider how the Holy Spirit in my mind will readjust time in order to assist me with my mission while I am here in the dream of form, together with all others. You see, for me to achieve my purpose, someone else must first achieve their purpose, and so on. There must be an adjustment in time for the miracle of past error to be turned into knowledge.

Therefore, what now does time mean, other than for defeating my own fears and allowing me to go beyond them, where reality holds my holiness, just as it holds yours? This is where no two minds can join in the desire for truth, without Truth joining them.

Chapter 44
Don't Give Him What He Doesn't Ask For

Truth cannot join us anywhere in the past or future, because neither exists. Only in our separated and fragmenting, dreaming state are past and future a thought. Eternal oneness has no clue of any such awareness. The past is only what you thought it was, and the future is only what you think it might be. Both are unreal.

Anything real can only be here, *now*, in this instant, and then it is gone and a brand-new instant is immediately born. Think about those glorious moments you've had when you had no thoughts of past or future, such as those timeless moments during sex, or dancing, or total engagement in joyous, thoughtless "flow"-type activity. We all have experienced peak-level moments, without any influence of diving into the past or predicting the future.

For example, this particular writing session began at 5:30 AM and it's now 7 AM, an instant in reality where clock-time has no meaning. Sure, there was the background interference of the prison environment, but it was *nothing* that could interfere with my mission at hand during the instant of real time, which is no-time.

Only in these instants, when you are determined to see the ego for the nothingness it is, will you accept the Holy Spirit as the presence of your mind that exists *now*. How long is an instant? It's the length of time it takes you to choose, and live inside, the Holy Spirit's right-minded thought process, over the wrong-mindedness of the ego, plagued with guilt. In these instants you meet your own holiness.

Each instant is a clean and crystal-clear, untarnished new birth of thought, and is your glimpse of eternity. Eternity never sees the past or touches the future, but is always in this instant, *now*. When an impure thought strikes you, in that instant ask the Holy Spirit to replace it with pure, right-mindedness. He will never fail in delivering this to you in a holy instant.

A Fresh New Instant

A holy instant is where your willingness strikes, to allow the next instant to arrive, and so on. Preparing your mind for the holy instant is to simply recognize within yourself that this is where you want to live. It's not at all necessary for you to do more now to have what you desire in the future. Rather, try to realize that there is nothing more you can do. Trying to do more takes your mind away from this instant and gives the Holy Spirit what He has not asked for.

You must always be operating from this very instant, *now*; *whoops*, it's gone, and now you're in a fresh new instant.

By giving the Holy Spirit any thought outside of this instant, you add the ego to Him and confuse the two. Your desire to live your own free will is all that He asks for in this instant. He will always be telling you what to do next in the instant to follow, and so forth. He joins with you because He is you, in this instant, to make each successive instant far greater than you can imagine.

Try it, right now; it works. In other words, don't take leaps forward without contemplating, but enjoy the step you are on now. If there is no joy or pure thought, ask in that instant for it to be corrected.

In his book *The Power of Now*, Eckhart Tolle asks the reader to practice this while, say, on a flight of stairs. Take each step as a new "now," and when reaching the end of the stairway notice that this is not the future, but rather is "now." So with that understood, how long is an instant? It's the time it takes to toss the ego aside and have the knowledge "now" that you have entered a holy instant.

Don't confuse your holiness of this tiny ego-free instant with any notion of smallness, however. Humility, yes, but your holiness does not ask that you be content with less than greatness. My own difficulty in seeing the holy instant as mine was in the conviction that I didn't deserve it until my past errors were repaired or repented. But what I didn't realize was that those errors were forgiven in an instant, and the Holy Spirit began in that instant to use time within the dream to undo my past.

Once the past was let go, I began seeing a new desire that created enthusiasm, which created inspiration, for a purpose that

I started perceiving as a necessary step for living my own chosen true free will. All of this came about in tiny instants, and as I write these words for you *now*, it's another instant, and of course you will read each word in an instant that's right for you, followed by further instants. *A holy instant*, for certain.

Don't Confuse Your Role with His

Your willingness to live your free will is delivered to you within an instant and comes from God's Will. He did not create you within Himself only for you to be unworthy. With this accepted and realized, if you do not enter where He wills you to be, you are interfering with His Will.

Compared to God, your willingness alone is little, but combined with His unlimited power it brings you the results the Holy Spirit has pursued for you. Unlike another one of the ego's fear tactics, there is no need to prepare yourself for God. This would be an arrogant notion. You would be confusing your role with God's, and confusion like this just brings on more doubt and fear.

We will not find Atonement by thinking we must first atone, which means to undo. But you can offer your willingness to the Holy Spirit, so He can proceed with His methods for undoing your errors. Remember, your errors are merely an instant—wrong-minded thoughts that sink you deeper into the dream of time and separated minds. After all, this is why God has placed His Holy Spirit in your right-mind. Your pure thoughts are of God alone and are communicated into you by the Holy Spirit.

So rather than trying desperately to prepare yourself for Him, try these following thoughts during your favorite meditation technique:

> I host God within me eternally, so I must be worthy of Him. He established His Home in me and created it to suit Him. It's not necessary that I make it ready for Him, but only that I do not interfere with the plan He has for me, which is eternal. I have no need to add a single thing to His plan. But in order that I receive it I must be willing not to substitute my own plan in place of His.

That's all there is for you to think about. If you add more, you are merely taking away the little bit that is asked of you. Remember, we made guilt by trying to do too much, too quickly, which has made us fearful about not being able to accomplish our goals.

When we are out looking for love and preparing ourselves for it, we only add fear to the search. So release yourself to Him and do not assume His function. But be sure to give Him what He asks for, and you will see how simple and little your part is, and how great His is.

It always seems to be our decision alone to make everything that is natural and easy seem to be impossible. If you believe the holy instant is difficult for you, it is because you decided to believe what is possible and what is not. Give this instant *now* to your knowledge, and leave believing behind you. Once you accept your own knowledge, then accept another holy instant, where the past and future do not live.

The *Course* asks us to see it this way:

> Everything that God Wills is not only possible, but has already happened. And that is why the past is gone. It never happened in reality. Only in your mind, which thought it did, is its undoing needful.

Chapter 45
Your Naturalness Beyond the Dream

Each one of us has a responsibility to see the world through his or her own naturalness, without fear. Since dreams of fantasy are unreal, this is the process of *undoing what never was.* Your natural way is the first step toward your own free will, which is your purpose in this world.

This is the holiness that keeps us blessed together as the One Creation of God. No one loses and nothing is taken away from anyone. Everyone gains through this naturalness. Or, we can say the holy vision we each sustain is the naturalness of who we are. This way of living your life signifies the end of the sacrifice, because it offers everyone their free will. We're entitled to everything we truly want.

Your own naturalness not only stops the laws of the world in its tracks, but then reverses them to go beyond every restriction of time, space, distance, and limits of any kind. If you will study the true successes and achievements of many individuals, you will note that the laws of this world were against such progress.

Our ability to see beyond the ego-based ways is our holiness. Even if it's "rocket science," that reflection is the power of God being manifested through us.

Our Advances in Life

We've all heard it said before: "There is nothing the power of God cannot do." But the world you dream of has probably never told you that you are equal to His power in helping others. From time to time, when you feel a situation is difficult for you, or for someone else, simply enter a holy instant to include this thought for yourself or for helping a lost individual:

*There is nothing my holiness cannot do
because the power of God rests in it.*

Your holiness will always prevail with its glimpses of your true function in this world; this is why you are here.

These glimpses are a touchstone to your Truth beyond the dream of separation. If we already fully understood the difference between Truth and illusion, the Atonement would have no meaning, nor would it be necessary, and you wouldn't be reading this book. Our healing is the same as Atoning. The holy instant, the holy relationship, the Holy Spirit's methods of communication and healing, along with all the means by which awakening is accomplished would have no purpose. These are clearly aspects of the plan to change our dreams of fear to happy dreams, so we may easily, with calm and quietness of mind, comfortably reawaken to knowledge: the *Knowledge* of it all.

Remember, as we move through this final chapter, that all we experience is a mirrored reflection of our inner essence. Yes, it is difficult to not fully focus on our bodies as who we are. However, once I was able to realize and accept that my body is a projected image of how I see myself in this world, only then was I able to know that I cannot place myself in charge of this reawakening process. I'm not capable of distinguishing between my own advances and retreats.

What I mean here is this: I now see that my so-called self-made advances in life were actually efforts to retreat deeper into separation, or further into the dream. On the other hand, many of what I thought to be my failures, such as the errors that led me to prison, engendered essential advances toward seeing the real world.

The function of the holy instant is to remove all fear and hatred from our minds. The Holy Spirit will remove the guilt, allowing you to have this ego-free holy instant, simply by your asking Him—by showing Him your acceptance of His undoing force, and your willingness to forgive yourself.

I have seen my own little faith, joined with His understanding, which is my totality, help create my free will to begin its journey, and what has happened to me is unbelievable. He needs your true free will to be accomplished in order that the Atonement can be achieved with ease.

Nakita from Boston

On a particular day when I once again needed to have mail, a letter indeed showed up for me, postmarked from Boston. It was from Nakita. This was my sixth enlightening letter from her so far, this time written while on her business trip across the Atlantic Ocean. I sensed she wrote me these letters with the full intention of keeping me positive and focused—though the more "newsy" sections of her letters were always quite humorous and fun loving. In this letter, due to our language differences and some personal issues, I've done some editing.

Dearest Jim,

I want you to know there is a garden of minds extending its thought through Christ, and on to you, and the garden feels the glimmerings of love and hope that you hold. Your release from prison will be soon, I am certain. I also have been seeing much about prison reform on the news for Ohio. Many are behind you, so please hang in there, for us. I am including a gift of words, which I hope will help you at times of despair and anxiety and fear. They are my words I share with you, so now this means they are your words too, Jim. Here are *our* words:

I desire this holy instant for myself, that I may share it with my brother, who I love with God. It is not possible that I can have this holy instant without you, or you without me.

Yet it is wholly possible for you to share it with me whenever you would like. And so I now choose this instant as the one to offer to the Holy Spirit, that His blessing unites us and keeps us both in peace.

I so much look forward to hearing from you whenever you would like...

Truthfully in peace with you,
Nakita

Finally, but with minimal details, Nakita answered my question as to how she ever came to find me. She explained that about six months before, on her first trip to Boston to meet with an international law firm, she stopped on her way to visit New York City. She had always wanted to see more of the city.

Over her five-day visit in New York, Nakita wanted to attend Sunday services in a neighborhood Catholic church. She asked a casual passerby while visiting Staten Island, and this nice man directed her to St. George's

Parish.

During the mass she noticed a prayer list in the holder on the back of the pew in front of her. The list had names of people with different situations of suffering, like illnesses and other hardships, and "me" as a prisoner. Yes, my name was on this prayer list in a church in Staten Island, where I was born, but left for Ohio with my parents when I was *three months old.*

I did a double-take in disbelief and actually commented aloud, "Aww, come on! No way!" I then proceeded to read further. And then looked away and said, "Holy Christ, what is this?" But she, Nakita, my friend, showed me her honesty in this.

While Nakita was looking at the prayer list, a couple sitting next to her realized she was an unfamiliar presence at the church. The woman, who was seated next to Nakita, quietly pointed to my name on the list and whispered that her husband had been writing letters to me. The husband looked over to Nakita and smiled to concur. Interested, Nakita asked the couple to tell her more about me outside the church after mass.

The two conversed with Nakita while escorting her to the parking spaces, then stopped at the couple's car. The husband retrieved his briefcase from the backseat of the car, where he had stored a copy of a recent letter from me to him. He neatly ripped off my return address and gave it to Nakita.

The husband, Joel, the world-class cello player I wrote about earlier in this book, made a slight reference to my interest in *A Course in Miracles,* for whatever reason, during their conversation about why I was in prison. Of course "slight" is all he knew; I had never expanded on the matter to Joel.

But whatever it was I had briefly mentioned must have stuck like glue in his mind. I do remember closing a letter to him with a brief quote from the *Course.* That's all. I didn't want to push the *Course* on him. My intention was only to pass along a healthy, healing quote. Now I could see it all unfolding. I was learning more and more, naturally, about wholeness and how it finds us.

Let me add that Joel is a principal cellist—of twelve cellists—for a large symphony orchestra. In performance, the cellists keep their focus on the principal and his movements. Joel, as the principal, is the one cellist who keeps his focus on the conductor. This is how they stay in unison.

As I rested on my top bunk, flat on my back, I was in awe. Motionless. I then read on in her letter about how the meeting in Boston had something to do with a World Center for Peace and Wellness on her property, which would educate and help the homeless, among other programs. A portion of her many acres in the hills, several miles outside of Split, Croatia, was destined to be a successful model for peace and forgiveness—and for fun, too, she added. She then asked if I enjoyed skiing or golf. (!)

Nakita was limited and careful, it seemed, in her description of the plans, as if she didn't want to "let the cat out of the bag" too soon. She did extend an open invitation for me to visit someday, and she insisted that day would be soon. Her loving message deeply touched me and was a soothing balm to my life under the oppression of prison. I felt a rush of energy that warmed me inside, as if I were blushing all over, and my eyes filled with tears. It was a sensation of belonging to something incredible, the highest grandeur ever. It was the same feeling I had on the night of the worldwide meditation. It was good, and I knew it. A holy relationship was being brought forward in my mind. This was real, and was only ever special in the dream.

Being Natural

Any holy relationship we develop is a creation blessed with every holy instant we experience, which brings the relationship together and will result in many others joining the Atonement. How so? you ask. Because the thoughts are ideas that extend inward to reach the minds of others. But do we actually plan this out?

Of course not. It is because God's Will wants it to be so. The means to the whole process belong to Him and are not our doing individually, but we are at-one with it. Once you accept the purpose that is your free will, He will with certainty provide the means necessary. The means will always be provided for anyone who shares in His Will.

His Will gives us happy dreams of love that come true because they've always been true. You've had them blocked by guilt. Their message is that of naturalness, rather than being urged or forced into place. Of course the alignment of the means to purpose is a Divine undertaking we find difficult to understand, much as we are not able to dissect naturalness, but do know that it is what it is. It is Truth.

Often we don't even realize we have accepted the Holy Spirit's purpose as our own, and usually wind up bringing unnatural, or unholy, means to gain its accomplishment. This is where the errors arrive onto the scene, which the Holy Spirit will undo. The faith in our naturalness is all that is necessary to receive the means and use them for living out our true free will, while we dream.

To love yourself, as well as to love your brothers/sisters, is the Oneness of the entire Sonship and is not of the dream. It's not fantasy, is natural, and has nothing to do with the body. But it will reflect through the body as the dream plays out. Your holy relationships are as natural as your loving your brother, sister, and yourself. This is so because love is one, and oneness is real.

Our special relationships are formed in the dream, but of course can often develop into holy relationships. Many times they do not. Yet even when the special relationship does not become holy, it is used by the Holy Spirit, who has a special purpose for it that you may never become aware of.

Just stop and think about how many times that loving relationship you had was the result of a temporary, nonlasting relationship of the past. The Holy Spirit may directly or indirectly make happy dreams from that once-special relationship that never amounted to much. These happy dreams spread joy to others, who believe that love is fear and not happiness. Allow Him to fulfill the function He gave to your relationship by accepting it for you, and nothing will be deprived that would make it what it is not intended to be.

If you feel the naturalness of a relationship being threatened for any impure thought that may come along, however, stop for an instant and release that thought to the Holy Spirit. All you need to do is show the Holy Spirit your willingness, in spite of any fear, and let Him exchange the unnatural instant for the holy instant you would rather have.

Don't forget that your holy relationships are of Oneness, and impure thoughts are an antic of the ego, trying to agitate the Oneness you have knowledge of. That's all it is—so relax by having the attitude that whatever threatens the peace of one of you, the other can cast out. Your naturalness will cause the unholy to simply fade away.

The power in your understanding of this is a blessing you have given to the relationship without your ever realizing it. With this, you or your spouse, child, parent, friend, and all others you encounter will not experience fear alone, or attempt to deal with it alone. The fact that you understand what your brother/sister is dealing with means he/she is not alone. This is what Nakita and others have shown me and is the means given me to extend on to you the love and peace of the Little Garden Society, or Christ.

At one time, my own understanding of all of this faced questioning thoughts and challenges. But in an instant, an urging went through me to ask for answers. It was in another instant when I was answered, and then I knew my Abundance.

Resources

Castaneda, Carlos. *Journey to Ixtlan: The Lessons of Don Juan.* Touchstone, 1973.

The Foundation for Inner Peace. *A Course in Miracles.* Temecula, CA, 1975.

LaBerge, Stephen, PhD. *Lucid Dreaming.* New York: Ballantine Books, 1986.

Tolle, Eckhart. *The Power of Now.* Novato, CA: New World Library, 1999.

About the Author

Following tours of duty at Kent State University and in the U.S. Air Force, he spent the next twenty-five years in the financial services industry, excelling in a field he loathed – though not immune to its perks. By his thirties, running his own independent agency, he became an experienced public speaker and wrote a monthly column on financial security for Senior Forum, a regional Ohio newsletter. He then launched his own monthly client newsletter, Retirement Insights, which became hugely popular and evolved into a self-help publication with a nontraditional, nonreligious, spiritual slant.

Despite a long, successful career, in 2007 – faced with the pressures of an economy in freefall; the loss of one wife to cancer and two to divorce; the needs of his children and demands of an upscale lifestyle; and responsibilities to panicking clients – he illegally withdrew $100,000 of client's funds to try to recoup the value of their investments and rescue his floundering business. The strategy failed and landed him a sentence of ten years.

His time in prison has been hell, and has also been unexpectedly fruitful, resulting in his return to his first love, writing, and the series that begins with The Master of Everything. The manuscripts were painstakingly handwritten in lined notebooks (he has no computer available in prison) and the material just keeps on coming.

Books by James Nussbaumer

The Master of Everything
Published by: Ozark Mountain Publishing

Mastering Your Own Spiritual Freedom
Published by: Ozark Mountain Publishing

And Then I Knew My Abundance
Published by: Ozark Mountain Publishing

For more information about any of the above titles, soon to be released titles, or other items in our catalog, write, phone or visit our website:

Ozark Mountain Publishing, Inc.
PO Box 754, Huntsville, AR 72740
479-738-2348/800-935-0045
www.ozarkmt.com

Dolores Cannon
A Soul Remembers Hiroshima
Between Death and Life
Conversations with Nostradamus,
   Volume I, II, III
The Convoluted Universe -Book One,
   Two, Three, Four, Five
The Custodians
Five Lives Remembered
Jesus and the Essenes
Keepers of the Garden
Legacy from the Stars
The Legend of Starcrash
The Search for Hidden Sacred Knowledge
They Walked with Jesus
The Three Waves of Volunteers and the
   New Earth
Aron Abrahamsen
Holiday in Heaven
Out of the Archives – Earth Changes
Justine Alessi & M. E. McMillan
Rebirth of the Oracle
Kathryn/Patrick Andries
Naked in Public
Kathryn Andries
The Big Desire
Dream Doctor
Soul Choices: Six Paths to Find Your Life
   Purpose
Soul Choices: Six Paths to Fulfilling
   Relationships
Patrick Andries
Owners Manual for the Mind
Tom Arbino
You Were Destined to be Together
Rev. Keith Bender
The Despiritualized Church
Dan Bird
Waking Up in the Spiritual Age
O.T. Bonnett, M.D./Greg Satre
Reincarnation: The View from Eternity
What I Learned After Medical School
Why Healing Happens
Julia Cannon
Soul Speak – The Language of Your Body
Ronald Chapman
Seeing True
Albert Cheung
The Emperor's Stargate
Jack Churchward
Lifting the Veil on the Lost Continent of
   Mu
The Stone Tablets of Mu
Sherri Cortland
Guide Group Fridays
Raising Our Vibrations for the New Age

Spiritual Tool Box
Windows of Opportunity
Cinnamon Crow
Chakra Zodiac Healing Oracle
Teen Oracle
Patrick De Haan
The Alien Handbook
Michael Dennis
Morning Coffee with God
God's Many Mansions
Claire Doyle Beland
Luck Doesn't Happen by Chance
Jodi Felice
The Enchanted Garden
Max Flindt/Otto Binder
Mankind: Children of the Stars
Arun & Sunanda Gandhi
The Forgotten Woman
Maiya & Geoff Gray-Cobb
Angels -The Guardians of Your Destiny
Seeds of the Soul
Carolyn Greer Daly
Opening to Fullness of Spirit
Julia Hanson
Awakening to Your Creation
Donald L. Hicks
The Divinity Factor
Anita Holmes
Twidders
Antoinette Lee Howard
Journey Through Fear
Vara Humphreys
The Science of Knowledge
Victoria Hunt
Kiss the Wind
James H. Kent
Past Life Memories as A Confederate
   Soldier
Mandeep Khera
Why?
Dorothy Leon
Is Jehovah an E.T
Mary Letorney
Discover the Universe Within You
Diane Lewis
From Psychic to Soul
Sture Lönnerstrand
I Have Lived Before
Donna Lynn
From Fear to Love
Irene Lucas
Thirty Miracles in Thirty Days
Susan Mack & Natalia Krawetz
My Teachers Wear Fur Coats
Patrick McNamara
Beauty and the Priest

Other Books by Ozark Mountain Publishing, Inc.

Maureen McGill
Baby It's You
Maureen McGill & Nola Davis
Live from the Other Side
Henry Michaelson
And Jesus Said – A Conversation
Dennis Milner
Kosmos
Andy Myers
Not Your Average Angel Book
Guy Needler
Avoiding Karma
Beyond the Source – Book 1, Book 2
The Anne Dialogues
The History of God
The Origin Speaks
James Nussbaumer
And Then I Knew My Abundance
The Master of Everything
Mastering Your Own Spiritual Freedom
Sherry O'Brian
Peaks and Valleys
Riet Okken
The Liberating Power of Emotions
John Panella
The Gnostic Papers
Victor Parachin
Sit a Bit
Nikki Pattillo
A Spiritual Evolution
Children of the Stars
Rev. Grant H. Pealer
A Funny Thing Happened on the
     Way to Heaven
Worlds Beyond Death
Karen Peebles
The Other Side of Suicide
Victoria Pendragon
Born Healers
Feng Shui from the Inside, Out
Sleep Magic
The Sleeping Phoenix
Michael Perlin
Fantastic Adventures in Metaphysics
Walter Pullen
Evolution of the Spirit
Christine Ramos, RN
A Journey into Being
Debra Rayburn
Let's Get Natural with Herbs
Charmian Redwood
A New Earth Rising
Coming Home to Lemuria

David Rivinus
Always Dreaming
Briceida Ryan
The Ultimate Dictionary of Dream
     Language
M. Don Schorn
Elder Gods of Antiquity
Legacy of the Elder Gods
Gardens of the Elder Gods
Reincarnation...Stepping Stones of Life
Garnet Schulhauser
Dance of Eternal Rapture
Dance of Heavenly Bliss
Dancing Forever with Spirit
Dancing on a Stamp
Annie Stillwater Gray
Education of a Guardian Angel
The Dawn Book
Work of a Guardian Angel
Blair Styra
Don't Change the Channel
Natalie Sudman
Application of Impossible Things
L.R. Sumpter
We Are the Creators
Dee Wallace/Jarrad Hewett
The Big E
Dee Wallace
Conscious Creation
James Wawro
Ask Your Inner Voice
Janie Wells
Embracing the Human Journey
Payment for Passage
Dennis Wheatley/ Maria Wheatley
The Essential Dowsing Guide
Maria Wheatley
Druidic Soul Star Astrology
Jacquelyn Wiersma
The Zodiac Recipe
Sherry Wilde
The Forgotten Promise
Lyn Willmoth
A Small Book of Comfort
Stuart Wilson & Joanna Prentis
Atlantis and the New Consciousness
Beyond Limitations
The Essenes -Children of the Light
The Magdalene Version
Power of the Magdalene
Robert Winterhalter
The Healing Christ

For more information about any of the above titles, soon to be released titles,
or other items in our catalog, write, phone or visit our website:
PO Box 754, Huntsville, AR 72740
479-738-2348/800-935-0045
www.ozarkmt.com